A VERY
DIFFERENT LIFE

A VERY DIFFERENT LIFE

Maggie Thomson

To Andy and Jo who always make a plan.

Librario

Published by
Librario Publishing Ltd.

ISBN : 978-1-909238-01-5

Copies can be ordered from retail
or via the internet at :

www.librario.com

or from :

Brough House
Milton Brodie
Kinloss
Morayshire
IV36 2UA

Tel / Fax : 01343 850178

Cover design and layout by
Kings Design Studio, India

Printed and bound in Great Britain

CONTENTS

• SOUTHERN AFRICA •

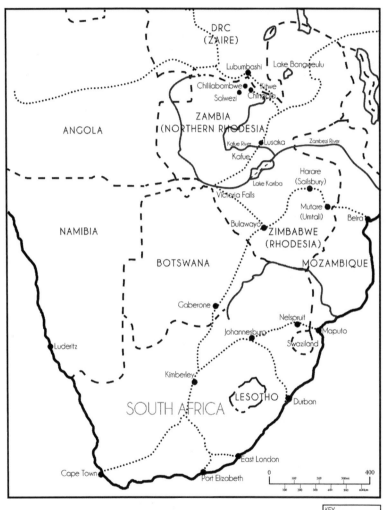

KEY
Main Rivers
Coast
Country boundaries
Railway

ACKNOWLEDGEMENTS

My story has been written in response to encouragement from family and friends in all four countries in which I have lived. I cannot list the many, many people who have given me help and support over the years. I thank you all from the bottom of my heart. You remain alive in my memories.

In the early stages Francis Kwari, Sheila and Mike Brown and Alex Fairall gave me invaluable advice and constructive criticism. Jo Onderstall has been a tower of strength, reading the manuscript many times and correcting my grammatical errors as well as encouraging me to publish. Helga and Nick Fry assisted me with the photographs as my computer skills are still somewhat limited. For the first time in 50 years I met up with Brian Collingridge, an old university friend, and he took the initiative to put me in touch with Mark Lawson, the Editor for Librario Publishers. Mark, in turn, has given me invaluable advice and support. Thank you all.

My final thanks goes to my family, most of whom have read the manuscript and given useful comments and encouragement. My grand daughter Claire assisted with producing the map. My special thanks to Andy and Jo who are always there for me. As a family we have faced many challenges together, working on the principle that it isn't what happens to you but how you handle it that matters.

May God bless and sustain you all as He has me.

*"Surely God is my help;
the Lord is the one who
sustains me."*

Psalm 54 v 4

INTRODUCTION

Christmas Day 1959

It is afternoon and here I sit on the stoep of my fiancé's parents' home, on a farm outside Lusaka in Northern Rhodesia. We have gorged ourselves on the mandatory turkey and accompaniments, and finished with the Christmas pudding in spite of the fact that the temperature is 28°C. Now the family has vanished to sleep off the surfeit of food. I am 22 years old and it is the first time I have spent a Christmas away from my parents, let alone on a different continent. As I look out at the banana and pawpaw trees, which are so new to me, I feel desperately homesick. Mac, my fiancé, is in the police and on duty far away which increases my feeling of loneliness.

"Are you feeling sad, Maggie?" It is Ouma, Mac's granny. "Come on, I will cheer you up. I will tell your fortune!" and off she bustles into the house. I know the family teases the old lady about being psychic so it will be a bit of fun, not to be taken seriously.

She returns with a pack of cards which she lays out and from which she asks me to choose, then she begins. She tells me various things which she already knows, that I am an only child of loving parents and so on, then she says –

"You are going to be seriously ill to the point of death, and it will happen twice." I laugh as I am the picture of health.

She continues, "Two people who are very close to you will come and take you back to England," then, frowning, "there are two men in your life who will cause you great pain."

Finally she says, "In spite of all this you will be immensely blessed."

Given where I am in my life at this time with my future planned these predictions seem no more than rather grim fantasies to pass a sunny afternoon. As night approaches the crickets and tree frogs start chirping and the family gathers again for sundowners in the cool of the evening. So ends my first Christmas in Africa.

Four months later some of Ouma's predictions begin to come true and she is so shaken that she never tells another fortune.

This is my story.

" There is a time for everything, and a season for every activity under heaven."

Ecclesiastes 3 v 1

When would I ever see them again? Was I doing the right thing? I knew only one person in the whole continent of Africa. Was I being selfish? My father had said that if I loved them I wouldn't go, but that wasn't true. All these questions tortured me as I stood at the rail of the *Capetown Castle* watching the gangplanks raised as she prepared to set sail from Southampton for the ten-day journey to South Africa. Never, in a thousand years, could I have imagined the trauma that lay ahead.

I could see my parents waving and even at that distance knew they were in tears. I was their only child, and a cherished daughter, setting out for the unknown so of course they were anxious and upset. My emotions were in turmoil, torn between the sorrow of the present parting and the anticipation of the reunion with Mac after our year apart. We had met when we were both at Bristol University but he had failed his first year and had finally returned to his home in Northern Rhodesia (Zambia) and joined the colonial police force. Our relationship had not always been plain sailing. I remember going to meet him one day, having made up my mind to call off our romance. I cannot now remember what prompted that but when I arrived he was so warm and loving that my resolve failed me. I am sure that most of us have 'what if' times in our lives, and that was one of mine. It is pointless, however, to agonise about the past and while our choices in life may yield pain, the Lord can turn them into blessings.

My father was a very ambitious man and I doubt he would have considered anyone good enough for me. When I was fifteen I met Mike at the Weston cricket festival. He was tall, blonde and blue eyed with a warm outgoing personality and was my first love. My father forbade me from seeing him as I was at a private school and Mike was at the grammar school. 'What the eye doesn't see the heart doesn't grieve over' and we continued to meet in secret. I am not proud of my deceit but I am sure that our learning about the opposite sex together kept me out of trouble at university as I would otherwise have been very naïve. I am talking about the early 1950s and, unlike now, 'going all the way' was a non-starter. Mike is happily married and he and I have remained close friends.

When Mac failed at university he became unacceptable in my father's eyes and, in addition, he was a chronic asthmatic which was of great concern to my parents. Before he returned home he met with my father to ask if we could be married when I qualified and received an emphatic "No". We were very sad about the situation but were very much in love and I agreed to marry him. Shortly after he joined the police I received a parcel containing a hand painted model of the dwarf, Dopey, with instructions to break off his head! When I did, there was a solitaire engagement ring, wrapped in silver paper. I didn't have the chance to show it off then as we had agreed to keep out engagement a secret for the time being, in the hope that my father would relent. Now, on board ship, I could wear it openly for the first time.

Suddenly the brass band which had been blaring through the ship's loudspeaker softened to the refrain of *Will ye no' come back again*. It was just like a farewell in the worst type of tear-jerking film, and it worked. I sobbed. I still wonder why such music is always played as ships cast off, parting is usually painful and such accompaniment makes it almost unbearable.

There were three of us sharing our cabin. Elaine and I, both twenty two, and Maureen, an Irish girl, a few years older. On the dressing table there were flowers for each of us and a pile of mail which Maureen started to sort through when we had introduced ourselves.

"Where are you going?" she asked me.

"Northern Rhodesia" I replied.

"Which town?"

"Chingola."

"To do what?" she persisted.

"I am a teacher and have been posted to the high school there. I'm on contract with the federal government."

She gave a relieved laugh, "Oh, that explains why you have a letter from my husband!"

Her husband, Seth, was acting headmaster at the school and had written to welcome me to Africa. Maureen, meanwhile, was travelling out to join him as they had been married only a few months previously. Thus started an enduring friendship.

The boat journey was fun. We 'did' Las Palmas, tearing around in a taxi at breakneck speed and also buying some of the crochet work for which it is famous. As we approached the Equator we began to see flying fish and at night viewed the phosphorescence in the water behind the ship. Just before we were due to cross the Equator the purser came and asked if I would take part in the Crossing the Line ceremony and I agreed. The event took place by the ship's pool with Neptune in charge, decked in seaweed and carrying his trident. Only young females were his victims! We were individually charged and sentenced whereupon his attendants threw us into the pool and then proceeded to rub flour paste and smelly kippers into our hair! In spite of spending ages in the shower I seemed to smell of kippers for days afterwards.

Our arrival in Cape Town was on a cold, wet, windy morning and as the first glimpse of Africa it was not inspiring. We couldn't even see Table Mountain as it was covered in cloud. We were stuck in the customs shed for hours while the officers had great fun at our expense. As three young, obviously inexperienced, female travellers we were fair game for them. They refused to speak anything but Afrikaans with the result that we were last to be cleared and had to rush to catch the north-bound train.

That journey was long and tiring but also far more interesting than travelling by air. Just outside Cape Town we passed horrifying shanty towns, settlements such as we had never dreamed of. At that stage we were still untouched by the significance of racial problems in Africa. We were enthralled by the scenery as we set out through the Cape ranges. Arum lilies grew wild in the valleys and the mountains rose up bare and beautiful. There were Dutch-style farmhouses, sparkling white, nestling in vineyards with everything looking so peaceful and well tended. As the journey progressed and we settled down, the country became flatter, drier, trees fewer and sheep more numerous. We were crossing the Karroo and the scenery was monotonous so we turned our attention to playing cards. A short stop in Kimberley broke the routine as we had a brisk walk in town but, for all its diamonds, it was disappointing.

The meals on the train were excellent and full of interesting new foods. 'Snoek' turned out to be tasty fish, and 'squash' a delicious vegetable of the marrow family, about the size of an orange. Fresh fruit included guavas and pawpaws which were then new to us. Everything was strange and exciting and of course sleeping on the train was a new experience.

The air became hot and dry and we all felt parched as we crossed the edge of the Kalahari Desert where there was not a tree in sight. Slowly it changed, bushes began to appear and flat-topped thorn trees became more numerous as we approached the Rhodesian border. All along the way mail was delivered and collected without even stopping. The train slowed down, a guard threw out a mail bag and then wielded something like a large butterfly net to pick up the bag of incoming mail. That bag was then left for sorting at the next stop.

Our next long stop was Bulawayo where Elaine left us as she was going to Salisbury (now Harare). I was met there by two teachers who took me back to their house for a meal and, most welcome of all, a bath. They made me quite apprehensive about travelling North of the Zambezi River with tales of malaria, blackwater fever, sleeping sickness, putsi fly larvae that burrow into the skin and jigger fleas that live under toe nails. I started the last leg of the journey with grave misgivings about what I was letting myself in for. I really did not know what to expect. Although I had an honours degree in geography we had never studied Africa apart from some consideration of the climates and vegetation.

At Victoria Falls station I was very touched to find some friends of my parents waiting to drive me to see the falls. I cannot begin to describe the wonder of the sight. Subsequently I have visited them many times and am always filled with awe. They underline the insignificance of man against the wonders of nature. The view of the Zambezi, which is almost two kilometers wide at that point, plunging for 120 metres, is breathtaking. It is said that at peak flow 120 million gallons of water a minute crash downwards and the noise is deafening. The Tonga name for the falls is *Mosi-oa-tunya* which means 'the smoke that thunders,' a very appropriate description as the spray rises high into the sky so that when approaching from a distance it looks like smoke from a bush fire. The thundering of the crashing water seems to make the earth shake and below the falls the Zambezi bubbles and foams as it rushes downstream.

Watching over the falls on the Zambian side is the statue of David Livingstone who was the first white man to record their existence. Here was my first sight of baboons in the wild. There were notices on the paths warning visitors not to feed them as they could become vicious. All too quickly I was taken for a hasty family breakfast and then back to reboard the train at Livingstone.

On 9th August 1959 we reached Lusaka and there was Mac to meet me. I had been invited to spend a fortnight with his parents on their plot just outside the city and he had taken leave so that he could show me some of the country he loved so much. Being with him again was like a dream come true we just couldn't stop gazing at each other, hugging and kissing. There was just so much to share that we went and had a cup of coffee before setting out for the farm. I dreaded meeting my future in-laws but they were kindness itself and immediately took me into their home as a daughter. Jim, Mac's father, still had his Scot's accent after 50 years in Africa. His mother, Joan, was born a South African but had none of their nasal speech. They gave me my first taste of the sort of hospitality that is found in Africa. Everyone seemed easy-going and always with a well-stocked larder for unexpected visitors. In later years I also learnt to be prepared and not to get flustered by the unexpected arrival of a large family for the weekend. Of course it was easier than in Britain as domestic workers bore the brunt of such occasions.

The weather in much of southern Africa encourages outdoor entertaining as there is little if any rain for about six months of the year. I was introduced to a *braaivleis* which is the South African form of a barbecue. After a hot day there can be few things more pleasant than sitting out in the cool of the evening, grilling meat on an open fire and drinking the inevitable cold lager. A *braai* is also easy entertaining for the womenfolk as, traditionally, the men do the cooking. South Africans are prodigious meat eaters, probably dating from the pioneer days when there was plenty of game.

Those first two weeks flew past. I was introduced to the farm workers as Mac's wife as the significance of being engaged was completely foreign to African culture. Mac was asked how much he had paid for me and when he said "nothing" there was much alarm. "Couldn't the Bwana find a good virgin?" was the question.

Mac promptly countered with "I was only teasing. I had to pay four cows," and everyone was satisfied.

One evening, a couple of days after my arrival, there was a commotion outside the house. The workers had come to give me a ceremonial welcome which involved singing and dancing. There can be little that is more moving than listening to African men harmonising. It was also my first introduction to the ululating of the women which is a sound denoting praise or celebration. It is produced by a high pitched hoot with the hand moved backwards and forwards in front of the mouth so that it sounds like yodelling. The noise is so uninhibited that it creates a sense of excitement. The dancing was very explicit and involved much hip thrusting which made me blush.

Everything was so new and exciting. Mac was a keen angler and gave me lessons in fishing on the Kafue River. The main fish we caught were black barbel or catfish. They are very ugly and not good eating as the flesh tastes muddy but the workers on his parent's plot relished them. It was on these fishing expeditions that I first saw hippo in the wild. On one occasion we had to beat a hasty retreat as two of the great animals, more curious than the rest, started making a bee-line for us. They are very dangerous and definitely best avoided.

The bush in August is extremely dry and we had some drama when a bush fire started to sweep relentlessly across the farm. The flames were treetop high, or so it seemed. The whole family and the workers turned out to fight the blaze and protect the field of Turkish tobacco. Huge egrets, gliding overhead, enjoyed the feast of insects that the fire put up while we beat it with branches and became hot, smoky and soot stained. This was the Africa that I had expected from films I had seen and when I arrived in Chingola it was rather an anticlimax at first.

The wealth of Northern Rhodesia (Zambia) depended on its copper and it had the richest ore in the world as well as one of the largest open pits. To my amazement Chingola was a thriving modern town. The government supplied accommodation and I discovered that I had travelled to Africa only to live in a block of flats. What a let down! In fact the houses are almost exclusively single storied bungalows which I have since had cause to appreciate. The shops were well stocked and, to my surprise, everything could be bought 'on account' with a substantial discount for cash. This even applied to groceries and it effectively discouraged budgeting. Well-paid miners just settled up at the end of the month and often lived beyond their means because of this system. As civil servants we were always the poor relations of the community and kept strictly to cash.

My flat mate was Marion, the domestic science teacher at the school. What an ill-assorted pair we were! She was born and brought up in Northern Rhodesia and was convinced that the English in Africa only came to challenge the white residents on racial issues. She was also very organised and houseproud whereas I tended to be easy-going and rather disorganised. She was horrified to return one weekend and find three ducklings roaming the bathroom, two rabbits in a cage in the kitchen and a tiny kitten investigating everywhere. Fortunately they were in transit to Mac so we remained friends although I must have sorely tried her patience.

Our flat was very large and modern with furniture supplied by the government. We employed a 'houseboy' called Cigarette to do the laundry and polish the cement floors. Dealing with an African servant was difficult at first but I soon discovered that he had a lively sense of humour and would happily carry out any request made with a smile. Marion disapproved strongly of my approach but I still believe that a friendly smile achieves much more than a frown.

Chingola High School was a European co-ed school occupying a large, airy, double- storey building. Many of the pupils were South Africans and Afrikaans was their first language. Often the classes dissolved into laughter at my attempts to pronounce their names. In the first week I gave the senior class a quick test on work that they had covered in the previous term and asked them to write their age at the top of the paper. As quick as a flash one of the boys came back with, "Sorry miss, I've got a girlfriend already!" It was my first experience of teaching boys and, as many of them were only a couple of years younger than I was, I had to keep my wits about me. They took great delight in trying to make me blush and often succeeded.

The academic day started at 7.30 and ended at 12.45 to avoid the worst of the heat. Every day I would arrive in my classroom to find, on my desk, either a rosebud or a gardenia and a pin so that I could attach it to my dress. I soon learnt to pin a rose in front of the shoulder but a gardenia at the waist as the perfume could be overpowering. It was a lovely thought at the beginning of the day. I wonder whether such things happen anywhere in the world these days.

Although academic teaching finished at lunchtime the school day was far from over. The afternoons were occupied by sporting activities. I had played second team tennis at school and first team hockey at school and university so did a course at university, in my post-graduate teaching certificate year, which qualified me to teach games. As a result I found myself coaching hockey or tennis in temperatures of 27° C and over. Teaching swimming in the Olympic-size mine pool was no hardship as I invariably joined my charges in the water.

When I was at school in England I studied speech and drama which I really loved. Not only did I participate in school plays but a group of us set up our own drama club and produced some plays in the church hall. Two of my friends from those days went on to RADA (Royal Academy of Dramatic Art) and became professional actresses. Mac's brother, Jimmie, lived in Chingola and introduced me to Doug, who invited me to join the dramatic society and I leapt at the chance. Apart from anything else it gave me the opportunity to meet different people. I had a small part in a one act play and then was cast as the leading lady in the Chingola production for the Northern Rhodesia Drama Festival. There were only three of us in the cast, two men and me, so there was a lot to do and rehearsing took up most of my evenings.

Weekends were special because, if we could organise lifts, either I went to where Mac was stationed in the bush at Solwezi, or he would come into town. Solwezi was a very small centre in the bush, 105 miles from Chingola on a bad dirt road. I loved it because it was out in the wilds. I used to stay with Mac's officer-in-charge and his wife, John and Lil. A very happy memory from those days is walking in the bush early in the morning, hand in hand with Mac. The grass was about five feet tall and festooned with cobwebs laden with dew. As the early sun's rays caught them everything seemed to sparkle and shimmer. Magical.

I was young, very much in love and excited by my vision of the future, the only black cloud on the horizon for me was my father's continued refusal to accept Mac. I had written to tell my parents that we would be getting married in August and my father had replied at length saying that if I went ahead I would no longer be his daughter. I was deeply saddened by all this, not just for myself but also for my mother. He was so strong and determined that she would never be able to stand up against him. I loved and respected him and understood how his childhood had influenced his attitude.

My father was the eldest of a family of nine, two of whom died young. When he was 13 his mother died and he had to leave school. He worked in the Cornish clay pits during the day and then helped to run the farm on the edge of Bodmin Moor in the evening. With all that he also went to night school and by the time he was 21 he had managed to save the fifty pounds necessary to join the Prudential Assurance Company where he was soon their youngest district manager. With that behind him it was not surprising that social position and financial security were of major importance to him. I found it hard to subscribe to the same values as I had such a different upbringing. Like most parents he tried to give me the advantages that he never had in his childhood.

My mother suffered pre-eclampsia when I was born and as a result it was decided that I should be her only child. In today's world it is assumed that an only child is spoilt but I would beg to differ on that. All too often an only child is also a lonely one and, not having the rough and tumble and squabbles with siblings, does not learn to stand up for herself. An only child is also often the sole repository for her parents' hopes and dreams, as in my case, and it can be very stressful. As my life turned out I have felt the lack of siblings more as I have grown older but I have been blessed with wonderful friends.

I had a very strict upbringing with my father being the dominant force in my life. My mother was a quiet and gentle lady who allowed him to dominate her as he also did in most aspects of my childhood. He never laid a finger on me but I was always a little in awe of him and craved his praise even when I began to rebel against his possessiveness and dictatorial ways. He would often describe me as stubborn and, in retrospect, he was probably justified. In many ways we were similar which probably accounted for the way we clashed as I grew older.

"All the days ordained for me were written in your book before one of them came to be."

Psalm 139 v 16

Friday 8ᵗʰ April, 1960

Today started just like any other. I woke at 6.30 am as usual and had a slice of pawpaw for breakfast before the ten-minute walk to school. Last night I burnt the midnight oil and finished writing all the school reports for my class so am feeling quite tired but now I can really start looking forward to the weekend. At two o'clock Ken will come to pick me up and we will drive to Solwezi to fetch Mac as he is to be best man for his brother Jimmie's wedding tomorrow. Ken is my leading man in the festival play so we shall be able to practice our words on the journey and the time will soon pass. When we return Mac's parents will have arrived from Lusaka and we will all have dinner together. I have bought a new dress for the wedding and a beautiful pair of shoes with 2½ inch heels. It is all so exciting to be involved in a family event like this.

I will have a short nap on my bed before Ken arrives.

Monday 11th April 1960 – three days later

I don't remember turning the radio on.

I haven't heard that advert before.

I must be dreaming.

Perhaps I should get up now, Ken will be here soon.

I open my eyes and see my parents by my side but it isn't my bed so I know I must be dreaming as they are in England.

I close my eyes again.

I am being buried alive!

Something is being put over my back and I can't move.

Suddenly I feel myself spin onto my back and a weight is being taken off the front of my body.

I open my eyes again and there, hanging from a bar over my bed, is a wedding bouquet of beautiful Eucharist lilies.

My parents and Mac are there at my bedside.

Now, for the first time I know something is wrong.

Where am I?

How did I get here?

I don't seem able to move and my head feels strange.

Everywhere around me seems to be covered with flowers, a mass of colour which almost hurts my eyes.

My mother is crying.

It all seems too much.

I go back to sleep.

I don't know how long I slept but I was later told that I had been unconscious for two and a half days. When I woke it was to hear another lady in the ward playing her radio loudly which probably explained the advert that I didn't recognise. My parents and Mac told me I had been in an accident just outside Solwezi.

I still have no memory of the event but Ken told me later that I had offered to drive his VW Beetle for the last fifty miles. It was a fairly bad dirt road and I had never driven a front-wheel drive vehicle before. Apparently a lorry was parked on a left-hand bend and I skidded as I overtook it,

I corrected the skid then collected another one, over-corrected and the car rolled three times. This was before the days of safety belts and I was thrown out of the car, which rolled over me. Ken remained in the car and sustained two cracked ribs but I broke my back and fractured my skull. I have always been thankful that it was not Ken who sustained the serious injuries as I was the one driving.

The driver of a Land Rover found us and managed to lift me and sit me up in the back of his vehicle to take us into Solwezi. Mac was out on farm patrol but his officer-in-charge, John, sent for his wife, Lilian, who was a retired nurse and, as the Provincial Nurse was away from the station, had a set of emergency keys for the clinic and the drug cupboard. She suspected back injuries as I was thrashing about in pain above the waist but didn't move at all below. She had me laid flat and strapped to two mattresses before finding the strongest drug available to relieve my pain and stop me moving. I was then loaded onto a canvas backed Government vehicle for the 100-mile dusty drive to Chingola. Ken and the African driver sat in the front and Lilian stayed at my side in the back. She told me subsequently that she doubted that I would reach Chingola alive as my blood pressure was dangerously low.

Chingola Hospital serves Nchanga Mine and when the staff realised that I was teaching in the government school they would not admit me but sent us a further forty miles to the new government hospital in Kitwe which later proved to be a blessing.

John meanwhile, had the unenviable task of telling Mac what had happened and arranging for him to drive to Kitwe and also to phone my parents. Only later was I told all that occurred from the time I lay on my bed in my flat until I woke in hospital.

Llewellyn Hospital had only recently been opened and was well equipped. The staff had found a Stryker bed for me which consisted of two canvas stretchers and a frame. I lay on one stretcher which was covered with pillows and, when it was time to turn, pillows were placed on top of me and the other stretcher fixed over them. At the turn of the handle at the bottom of the bed the whole contraption spun through 180 degrees and the upper canvas and pillows were removed. In this way I was turned sunny side or bottoms up every three hours. This explained why I thought I was being buried alive in my semi-conscious state! As a result of this bed I never had a trace of a pressure sore which is the dread of those who are bedridden.

In the five weeks that I was in Lewellyn Hospital I was injected with omnipon, a derivative of morphine, and consequently suffered very little pain. My main complaint was a very itchy stomach. When I was admitted internal injuries were suspected so the surgeon opened me up to check and Elastoplast was put over the site of the operation. I am allergic to Elastoplast and the itch nearly drove me mad but it also distracted me a little from the fact that I couldn't feel or move my legs. I concentrated hard on wriggling my toes but there was just no response which I found hard to believe as I had grown up with the philosophy that you can achieve most things if you really try. One morning I threw back the sheet and tried to sit up and get out of bed as I just hadn't grasped the fact that I had no movement or feeling in my legs. Strangely I dreamt night after night that I was walking barefoot through wet grass and could feel the blades between my toes.

The monotony of the days was broken by visits from my parents and Mac who were the only visitors allowed at first. Mac was able to come at weekends only. Twice a day I would hear my mother's high heels clicking down through the ward and my father speaking to other patients as they came to my bedside.

On one bad day I greeted my mother with "I should have died, it would have been better for everyone," and she replied, "You got to the gates my dear and St Peter said get down there Margaret Tremaine, you still have work to do." I have had reason to think of her statement many times since then.

Throughout my stay in Kitwe I received wonderful letters and flowers from my pupils although I had been at the school for only two terms. My 23rd birthday was spent in hospital and the kindness and generosity of those I had met in the eight months that I had been in the country was so heart warming and really encouraged me when things looked black. The hospitality of those days was demonstrated by a couple, Dick and Irene Draper, who lived near the hospital. I did not know them but they invited my parents to move out of the hotel and stay with them and became firm friends.

Visitors included people representing many different faiths and they were not always comforting. My parents were both brought up as Methodists so, in their childhood, chapel was a 'must' at least twice on a Sunday with no other activities permitted. The result was that my father was very dismissive of church declaring, "They are only after your money." Sadly his position on Christianity never changed. In spite of that I was sent to Sunday school from a very early age and read my Bible and Scripture Union notes daily. The private school that I attended was taken over by the Church of England and therefore we, as pupils, were more or less automatically confirmed at the age of twelve or thirteen. This event in 1950 was very meaningful for me although at that time little was said about the Holy Spirit. Subsequently my mother was also confirmed in the Church of England but neither she nor I could make any headway with my father in the matter of faith.

Being told by visitors that I would be healed if I had enough faith was not what I needed to hear at that time but of course lying immobile in bed means that one is a captive audience. A group of Sisters from the Convent of the Sacred Heart in Chingola came to see me regularly. On one occasion when they arrived I apologised for having been rather down on the previous Friday. One of the Sisters, who had grown up in the Bronx in New York, quipped immediately "Of course you were depressed, everyone is depressed on a Friday – it's fish day !" That made me smile but it was gentle Mother Alberta who gave me the greatest comfort. "Don't even think about it," she said, "Jesus understands exactly how you are feeling and you don't have to pretend to him or us." I have often thought about that.

After about three weeks my father told me that they had arranged for me to be flown back to England, to Stoke Mandeville Hospital, of which the spinal centre was world renowned. A nursing sister would fly back with us and care for me on the journey. Now a plaster of Paris cast was made in two halves, back and front of my torso, so that I could be turned on the journey. All this to be carried on a specially constructed frame made of Zambian teak.

About five o'clock on the morning of our departure I was bed bathed as usual and then I asked for my bed to be pushed out onto the balcony of the ward. May in central southern Africa is a lovely month. I lay there watching the sky turning from pink to gold to eggshell blue and wondered what the future held for me. A well-meaning visitor had said to me, "Swallow your pride, dear, go to Russia. I have heard that they have successfully grafted new legs onto rats so I expect they will be able to give you new legs." I thanked her for her concern, knowing that the problem was with my spinal cord not my legs. Nevertheless, surely with the miracles of modern medicine I would be healed at Stoke Mandeville and would still walk down the aisle at my wedding. How I prayed for that to happen.

For the present, I had to say goodbye to Mac, would I see him again? Would I see Africa again? So many uncertainties when five weeks previously it seemed that I had the world at my feet and a wonderful life ahead of me. Now I might be facing life as a disabled person. A quote by C. S. Lewis goes, "We ride with our backs to the engine….we have no notion of what stage of the journey we have reached….a story is precisely the sort of thing that cannot be understood till you have heard the whole of it." How true.

"God is our refuge and strength, an ever-present help in trouble."

Psalm 46 v 1

The plane journey back to England seemed endless. First we flew to Johannesburg where we changed planes and I was carried into the staff lounge to wait until we boarded for the last leg of the flight. The sister travelling with us gave me my last injection of omnipon somewhere over the Sahara. By the time we arrived at Gatwick airport the effect was wearing off and the ambulance journey to Stoke Mandeville was a nightmare as we juddered to a halt with monotonous regularity, presumably at traffic lights and stop signs.

The spinal unit was housed in converted army huts with each comprising a ward of twelve to twenty beds. When I had been transferred from the plaster cast into a bed the ward doctor came to talk to me. Doctor Michaelis became central to my life for the next six months during which time I came to appreciate his gentleness, understanding, and sense of humour. Almost my first words to him were, "Please can I have some omnipon, I am in agony?" Only to be told gently but firmly, "If we deaden your nervous system how will we know the extent of your injuries? You can have some aspirin." That was my introduction to Stoke.

The following morning there was considerable mirth amongst the staff on the ward and I was told that my plaster cast had been stood upright in a dark corner of one of the passages and had given several night duty nurses a fright. A male orderly from the men's ward then arrived to ask if he could have my wooden stretcher to make a coffee table as it was African hardwood. I was only too glad for it to be put to some use. Maybe someone is using that table today without knowing its history.

I arrived at Stoke late on Tuesday afternoon and Wednesday morning was Dr Guttmann's ward round. Sir Ludwig Guttmann, as he later became, was a short, plump, German Jew. He had pioneered, and was accepted as a world authority on, the rehabilitation of those with spinal injuries. He was invariably accompanied on his rounds by visiting doctors, physiotherapists and other medical personnel from all over the world, as well as members of his own staff. On Wednesday mornings everything had to be in apple-pie order. Any belongings were swept off the tops of lockers and we, the patients, more or less lay at attention with the sheets folded immaculately over us. Even the ward Budgie was incarcerated in a cupboard largely due to the fact that its party piece was to say "Hullo Poppa" which was the name by which Dr Guttmann was affectionately known.

I had been in the hospital for only about fifteen hours before the ward round but Poppa wanted to know from the physio why I wasn't already pulling a chest expander and why the occupational therapist hadn't already been to start me on something. He was very impressed by my general condition. "Here we have a girl (I was always a girl to him) who has been nursed in Africa for five weeks and she has no mark on her skin while we have patients from English hospitals who come to us with bed sores." I mentally thanked Llewellyn hospital and the Stryker bed. "But then," he added, "look at her tan, she has skin like leather."

After the ward round I had X-rays and then Dr Michaelis told me that he was going to do a lumbar puncture in order to get a more accurate picture of my condition. When he carried out the procedure he had a student nurse with him. He showed her the spinal fluid and said, "You see that it is all milky?" I had studied zoology at university and knew that it was a bad sign.

"I will never walk again will I?" I asked.

"I will never say never," he replied, "but let's say that you will only walk if there is a miracle, and I believe that miracles do happen."

"Will I be able to have children?"

He laughed, "My dear, you will have to worry about contraception just like everyone else."

The X-rays showed that my spine had fractured and dislocated at T 11 and 12 which were the lower thoracic vertebrae. In practical terms this means that I have no feeling or movement in my legs and no bladder or bowel control. It was decided that the dislocation should be treated by positioning my body in order to reduce it and then keeping me straight so that it could reset. It was 1960 and Dr Guttmann was against spinal operations which he deemed either unnecessary, or downright dangerous. With modern developments it might be different today.

For several weeks I had to lie with my body arched. When I lay on my back, rolled up pillows were placed under the small of my back, and when I was lying on my side my legs and shoulders were pulled back to keep me arched. At first the pain was such that I kept thinking that I should pass out and tears seemed to pour from my eyes although I was not actively sobbing. I believe that it is one of God's blessings that we cannot actually recall pain. I know that it was excruciating but I do not feel it again, whereas past joys can give a little surge of happiness when they are remembered. There was an arrangement of irises on the locker by my bed, and when I was lying so that I could see them, their very beauty somehow seemed to alleviate the pain. I cannot explain it but it was very real to me at the time, as though I could project the pain into them.

Day and night every patient was turned three-hourly in order to guard against pressure sores, I dreaded those turns. "Don't tense, it will only hurt more," I was told. How do you not tense when three male orderlies from the men's ward line up by the side of your bed, slide their arms under you and painfully heave you over? It was not only painful but also embarrassing as our requisite attire resembled a shirt worn back-to-front and just tied at the neck.

For the first few days I had a permanent headache which wasn't helped by an Italian orderly who sang *Volare* at the top of her voice. Visiting wasn't restricted and my mother stayed nearby for the first week. Pain is totally selfish and I was so possessed by it that it was much later before I was able to consider what my accident had meant to my parents. My mother was just grateful that I hadn't suffered brain damage but my father found my disability very hard to accept. He said later that if I had obeyed him and not gone to Africa the accident would never have happened but I knew that he was just expressing his frustration at not being able to change the situation. He started taking sleeping pills at the time and continued to take them for the rest of his life.

I was so blessed with visitors and in the six months that I was in Stoke someone came to see me every day which was wonderful. The day was also broken up by visits from the physio exercising my legs, and, when I was lying on my back, pulling the chest expander for 10 minutes every hour. The first few nights seemed endless as I was in too much pain to sleep and it was during those nights that I explained to God that I could do so much more for him if I could walk and lead a normal life.

I was just getting into the routine when Enid was put in the next bed to me and life took an upward turn. Enid and her family had been in a car accident which left her with a fractured spine. Before being transferred to Stoke her back had been operated on and the fracture stabilized by the insertion of a plate. At first we could only communicate when we lying facing each other or lying on our backs but it was so good to have a companion in the same boat and we soon became friends.

Enid was a nursing sister and had qualified at 'Barts' which was the same hospital where my mother's sister had trained. Auntie Nell had qualified in the early 1930s but they still found plenty to chat about. I teased Enid because, being one of the nursing fraternity, she had special blue china while I had hospital white.

Altogether Enid and I were in close daily contact for five months and we shared much soul searching about our situation. Enid is twelve years older than I and she had not had an easy life with her mother, father and brother all having died, whereas I had had a largely trouble-free life. In the hours that we spent sharing with each other I was really blessed by her wisdom and understanding. She was also a member of the Church of England and we received communion together. Quite difficult when lying 'bottoms up'! When we reached the stage of being allowed out willing parishioners pushed us to the Sunday service at a nearby church.

Enid's arrival helped immeasurably with the long painful nights as we used to do crosswords together, using a torch when the ward lights were dimmed, and whispering clues to each other. We were both avid readers and I frequently read a book a day. I still feel that access to the written word and the ability to read are immense blessings.

Enid was able to sit up and then get into a wheelchair about six weeks before me because her back was fixed with the plate, and how I envied her! Early on in my stay at Stoke Dr Michaelis said, "One thing that you will learn here is patience," but I am still struggling with it.

When I was first allowed to sit up after lying flat for over four months it was an enormous thrill. I can still see, in my mind's eye, a rather scruffy little tree and the grass around it which was my first view of the great outdoors after all that time. My joy was complete when I was able to drink a cup of tea without using a straw and eat my food without help. When being fed, it seemed to be very difficult to persuade a helper that I didn't want to eat all the cabbage, then all the carrots and so on. If I haven't learnt patience, I have learnt to thank God for all the things that we so often take for granted.

When I was first allowed out of bed my National Health wheelchair hadn't arrived so I had an ancient one. It really was like a padded armchair on wheels with wooden rims. When my own chair arrived it was like changing from a tractor to a Porsche. As soon as I was able, I wheeled to the bathroom and on my first visit dropped my comb. Sister Perks was passing the door so I asked her if she would pick it up for me.

"Pick it up yourself," was her reply.

"But I'll fall out of my chair!"

"Well, if you do there are plenty of people here to lift you back in again," was her rejoinder.

That was the philosophy at Stoke. We were told, "You are not ill, only disabled," and we were expected to help ourselves. At first it seemed hard but I think all old 'Stokites' would agree that it was the best possible way to prepare us for the outside world. Staff were not allowed to push us around the hospital and, as there was a long slope between the ward and the physio department we really had to work hard. Even visitors were liable to be ticked off if seen pushing a wheelchair.

Once out of bed I was brought face to face with the reality of incontinence. Until that time I had been catheterised and my bowels manually evacuated by a very practical Jamaican orderly. Now the catheter was removed and bladder training started. I have a spastic bladder which means that it contracts and empties itself at intervals. Whether with a spastic or flaccid bladder we were taught how to prompt it to empty by banging systematically on the front of the bladder region with the side of the hand. The toilet seats were covered with inflatable covers which were very necessary to avoid pressure sores as sometimes the process took a long time.

The first few times of manually evacuating my own bowels I found desperately humiliating but after a time I became philosophical about it. It is an aspect of being a paraplegic that most people don't realise. At Stoke we were all in the same boat so it was no big deal and the staff were always very supportive as they understood the emotional impact of these changes in our lives. Now it is just part of life, a matter of routine.

Now that we were mobile in our chairs, Enid and I spent a lot of time travelling from one activity to another. Enid already knew her way around so she acted as my guide. The main emphasis in our rehabilitation was building up strength in our arms because that was the route to independence. My arms were quite strong already which I attributed to the number of watering cans I had carried throughout my teens to water my father's tomatoes! At first physio consisted of strengthening exercises and learning to sit up straight on a bench without support which involved balancing from the waist and proved quite difficult. Then we moved on to archery which was a real challenge. My main problem was that I kept closing the wrong eye and then succeeded in hitting the target next to the one I was aiming at. After the first couple of sessions my aching arms certainly testified to the fact that it was an arm-strengthening exercise.

One big thrill was to go swimming as it was something I had always enjoyed. Getting into the pool was quite an exercise, involving a sort of chair lift which was swung into the water where the instructor helped us. It was very strange at first to be swimming with arms only. At one point I was swimming vigorously but getting nowhere and turned to find the instructor roaring with laughter and hanging on to my legs which of course I couldn't feel. Rather to my surprise my legs just floated as they were so relaxed. Freestyle was not on the programme as without the stabilising effect of kicking legs we rolled from side to side, so we concentrated on breaststroke and backstroke.

Physio was the main activity of the day. Having mastered sitting up without support, we moved on to standing and then walking with calipers. At first we exercised between bars and then moved away from them onto crutches. My physiotherapist was short and slim and I was terrified that she would not be able to support me if I fell. I was taller at five foot, six and a half inches and big-boned, but I soon learnt to trust her. The first method of movement was to put both crutches forward and then swing both legs through at the same time. The physio department echoed with thump, thump, thump as feet banged down and it was this sound that caused paraplegics to be nicknamed 'Plonkers'. The physios were referred to as the torture brigade but they did a wonderful job.

Once we were reasonably mobile we were allowed to go out with visitors. I remember clearly the first occasion that my parents collected me and took me out for a drive. It was early September and the countryside was looking beautiful. As we drove along, I thought to myself, "I couldn't pick that flower in the hedge, I couldn't walk across that field, I couldn't climb that tree." Suddenly it hit me how negative I was being – after all, when had I last climbed a tree? From that time I started to concentrate on all the things I *could* do.

I believe that the speed with which I adjusted to my disability was an answer to prayer. Many people were praying for my healing and I believe that their prayers were answered although not in the way that they had hoped. I know that I received inner healing which resulted in my coming to terms with what had happened. I believe that God could have healed me so that I could walk again but, in His wisdom, He had other plans for me.

Visitors continued to be a huge blessing. There were relatives, old school and university friends, and hospital visitors from different churches. One dear old lady used to bring Enid and me wafer-thin, cucumber sandwiches at tea time, and we were also spoilt with raspberries and honeycomb. With visitors willing to push, we could even have special dispensation to go to the local pub as long as we were back by nine.

About a week after I became mobile in my wheelchair the National Stoke Mandeville games were held. They were the precursor of the Paraplegic Olympics. I was only a spectator but Enid took part in the swimming and gamely pushed herself around in the 'wheel past'. Participants came from all over the country and there was an atmosphere of great excitement and of pride in being a Stokite. I chatted to one lady who had been disabled for 13 years and remember saying to Enid, "How dreadful !". Now I am writing this 50 years down the line.

Shortly before Enid left Stoke she and I were asked whether we would like to go to the Finmere Horse Show. We both leapt at the chance although we had a slight unease about toilet facilities there. We were the only two females in the party but decided to risk it. Off we went in the bus which was especially adapted to take wheelchairs. When we arrived there was no shortage of willing helpers and we were immediately taken off to the beer tent, only after a beer did we discover that there was no possibility of our managing the toilet! Men have a definite advantage in that respect.

The highlight of the day was the Donkey Derby in which famous jockeys rode. It was hilarious to see Sir Gordon Richards, Joe Mercer, Dick Francis and a host of others struggling to encourage their donkeys around the course. It was quite late when we set out for home and by that time the men were decidedly merry. They sang songs that I hadn't heard since travelling on coaches with the rugby team when I played hockey for the university. A very good time was had by all and as for the pool under my chair when we arrived back? Who cared? It was worth it.

Enid was discharged from the hospital at the end of August and I really missed her. I must have sorely tried Dr Michaelis' patience with my constant question, "When can I go home?" At long last the day dawned and on the 20th of October my parents fetched me and we drove to Weston-super-Mare. The icing on the cake was that two days after I returned home I was able to attend the wedding of Elspeth and Derek.

Elspeth was my closest friend – tall, slim, an extrovert and outstanding at sport, she was all I longed to be and I tended to remain in her shadow. In school holidays we, along with Mary, another friend, used to cycle around Somerset. Cheddar was a favourite destination in summer when there were strawberries to be had. It is sad that today it would not be considered safe for teenage girls to have so much freedom. We didn't have television so spent our leisure time playing sport, going on picnics or, when it was raining, which was frequently, reading and playing endless games of Monopoly or cards. Shopping was not a major option as our pocket money didn't extend to that. I feel so blessed that I have such a happy childhood to remember and attending Elspeth's wedding was a great joy. As our lives have turned out we see each other rarely but always pick up where we left off.

CHAPTER 4

" I can do everything through him who gives me strength."

Philippians 4 v 13

The house where I had grown up was definitely not wheelchair friendly. It was double storey with the bedrooms and bathroom upstairs so my bed was put in the lounge and I managed with a commode. For years my father had talked about buying somewhere different and now was the time. As a child I had the task of collecting mulberry leaves for the school silk worms from a tree belonging to an elderly couple who lived in a chalet bungalow nearby. Their house was on the market and, when my father explained my role in collecting the leaves, he had first refusal. The house had two bedrooms downstairs and Dad had one converted into a bathroom for me so that I was completely independent. What a pleasure !

The reality of living with a disability hit me hard when I returned home. These days counselling would be given after such a trauma but in those days one just got on with it. In retrospect I realise that I must have been very difficult to live with at first and I gave my mother a hard time. By nature I am a quick moving and independent person and I became incredibly frustrated especially if I had to ask for something to be done and it wasn't done as quickly, or exactly as I would have done it. I have learnt a lot over the years but I know that I still think of moving as quickly as I did at 22! A few years ago I was watching a hockey match and thinking how much I would love to play again. I was in my sixties at the time and then good sense prevailed as I realised that, disabled or not, I wouldn't be playing at that age.

For the seven and a half months that I was in hospital I was never alone and there was always someone around to lend a hand. When I returned home it seemed important to prove to myself, as much as to anyone else, that I could be independent. On one occasion my mother had pushed me into town on a shopping expedition. When we had finished I suggested that she should catch the bus and I would come home alone along the sea front. She was a bit anxious but I pointed out that the promenade was flat, after all Elspeth and I used to go roller skating there, and reluctantly she agreed. 'Pride before a fall!' What I hadn't realised was that there was a camber to the right so my right arm had to work twice as hard as my left. Nevertheless I made progress with frequent rests to let my arms recover. The distance was a little more than a mile and when I was half way disaster struck – I had a puncture. Now what? I was sitting contemplating my next move when our bank manager spotted me as he was driving home from work and came to my rescue. I realised then that independence has limits, not easy to accept when you are in your twenties.

In spite of the difficulties life did have its humorous moments. One day I decided to visit a friend on my own. All went well until I arrived, only to discover that I couldn't get to the front gate as there was a continuous pavement all along the road. I was contemplating this when along came an old man who had lived in Weston for years. He had a big three wheeler chair on which there was a bicycle chain and pedals which he moved with his hands. Both of us being disabled we began to chat and after a bit I told him about my quandary. "Don't worry my dear," said he, and proceeded to get out of his chair and push me up onto the pavement. I was totally dumbfounded. He then explained that he was a chronic epileptic which was why he had the chair. Life is full of surprises.

A few days after I returned home, a lady came to visit and said she had come to teach me to make dolls because, "You won't want to go far outside your house." I was shattered. "But I'm a teacher!" I replied in dismay. When my father heard the story and saw my distress he contacted a friend involved in education and a couple of weeks after my return I started teaching part-time at a nearby secondary modern school. At first I found it hard to teach sitting down as previously I had always moved around the classroom. It was also very different from teaching in Northern Rhodesia where there was stricter school discipline. In Chingola I would never have received a letter such as I had there, saying, "Please do not give Mary so much homework as it is interfering with us watching TV!"

As I came to appreciate more of the difficulties of my disability I felt that it was wrong to hold Mac to our engagement and wrote to him calling it off. He was adamant that he wanted to marry me so in the end we agreed that he should come to England for his three months long leave in March before making a final decision. My father now realised that I really loved Mac and said he would agree to our marriage if that was what we decided. Sadly he never came to terms with my disability. There is no doubt in my mind that it is more difficult to watch the suffering of someone you love than it is to suffer yourself, and with an only child the pain must be almost unbearable.

I anticipated Mac's arrival with both dread and longing but the minute we saw each other the past year seemed to vanish. We married on 22nd of April 1961 a year after the accident and it was a very blessed day, especially being surrounded by family and friends. There was a pain deep in my heart because I was not able to walk down the aisle which had been my dream but I had so much for which to be grateful. A friend made mud guards for the wheels of my chair so that my white lace wedding dress was spread out around me. The church was full, not only with invited guests but also well-wishers, which was so heart warming. To our surprise there were TV cameras outside the church. Apparently the marriage of a paraplegic was regarded as newsworthy. When we were on honeymoon a couple approached us to ask if we were the couple who married on TV.

Our honeymoon was a fortnight spent in Devon and Cornwall, our last experience of a wonderful English spring for many years. Back in Weston we packed up wedding presents and bought a car fitted with hand controls to take back to Africa. The days flew by and in early June Mac and I embarked on the *Pendennis Castle* liner from Southampton to Cape Town, bidding my parents another sad farewell.

"For I know the plans I have for you," declares the Lord," plans to prosper you, plans to give you hope and a future."

Jeremiah 29 v11

Life in our ship's cabin was complicated by the lack of space and called for a certain amount of ingenuity, to say nothing of a sense of humour. Fortunately we possessed both attributes and were aware early on that they would be vital in our life together. After we had been at sea for three or four days I began to suffer from nausea just when Mac was tucking into his kippers for breakfast. I put it down to being at sea in a wheelchair but when the 'sea sickness' continued every morning as we drove up the east coast of South Africa the truth dawned, I was pregnant. We had discussed starting a family after about two years but this was before the Pill, and the Lord had other ideas. I have had cause to be very thankful for that as my later life turned out.

Shortly after our return to Northern Rhodesia Mac was transferred to Chilanga as officer in charge. Chilanga is just south of Lusaka and is a small centre dominated by the cement works. The police station was brand-new and our house was situated next door, also new and surrounded by bush. Mac immediately started to plant a garden and we were given a lot of plants by his mother who was a very keen gardener.

One day there was a knock on the door and when I answered there was a lady with the kindest face who introduced herself as Gwen. Without a second thought I asked her to come in and have tea. She had stopped to ask whether she could give us any plants as she had seen Mac's efforts. We had an immediate rapport and she and her husband, Ted, became our closest friends. Ted shared Mac's love of fishing and they went off on many expeditions together while Gwen and I enjoyed each other's company. We used to go to Kariba together. The lake had just filled and Gwen and I spent hours swimming while the men fished. Now there are a lot of crocodiles and bilharzia in the lake so swimming is more hazardous. As I write in 2011 the brother of a friend has just lost his hand and forearm to a croc there, as he was trying to disentangle the boat motor from weed.

We had some very happy times in Chilanga. I was still relatively new to life in Africa and every day brought different experiences from the time the young police bugler sounded the 'Reveille' first thing in the morning, as the flag was raised, until he blew the 'Last Post in the evening. I was enlisted as a police reservist commissioned to teach basic map reading to junior officers. In addition I was taught to shoot with a revolver and was inordinately thrilled when I won a target-shooting competition.

The first present Mac bought me in 1961, when we were in Chilanga, was a electric sewing machine which I am still using. I put the foot control on the table and work it with my elbow which leaves both hands free. I still make most of my own clothes, particularly skirts as they need to be wide enough for me not to sit on them. When I buy blouses, they are usually far too long so I take them up and put slits in the sides so they can be comfortably be worn loose when it is hot. In the long run it is easier to make them myself. When my family visited from England they invariably brought lovely lengths of cotton material for me to sew. With Mac being in the police we were transferred fairly frequently and I spent a lot of time altering curtains – my least favourite sewing activity. That machine has paid for itself many times over.

Gwen and I went shopping in Lusaka once a week and I really enjoyed the outing. I had taken another driving test in order to prove that I could drive with hand controls. On one occasion a lady came up to me in the store and asked accusingly, "Are you pregnant?" When I replied, "Yes," her response was, "Downright disgusting I call it!" and she flounced off leaving me almost in tears with shock and anger.

The doctor decided that I should have a Caesarean section as the baby was in a breach position. At first I was very upset as I knew that I could have a normal delivery but in the long run the most important thing was that the baby was OK. On 16th February 1962, to our immense joy, Andrew was born. I was quite nervous at first as I had never held a young baby in my life but I guess that mothering skills are mainly innate. If I had any problems Gwen was there with advice. She had had four children and was a nursing sister trained in midwifery so understood my problems. Her presence and that of my mother-in-law helped to compensate for the fact that my own mother was so far away.

When Andy and I returned home we soon developed a routine which allowed me to do almost everything for him. Bath time was particularly well organised. David, our domestic worker and general factotum, put a chair by the bed and on it placed the bath with just enough warm water. Meanwhile I collected towels, nappy and clothes and put my feet up on the bed with the pram on the opposite side of my wheelchair to the bath. From there it was simple to lift Andy from his pram onto my lap, undress him, bath him, dry him on my lap, dress him and lift him back into the pram. When bath time was over David pushed him out to sleep under the thorn tree in the front garden. On the occasions when he was fretful it was not unusual to see a police constable marching up and down on the tarmac in front of the police station pushing the pram. In African culture babies are rarely left to cry.

The sister in charge of the maternity ward, a Scottish spinster, had told me in no uncertain terms that my baby should sleep through the night by the age of three months and so he did. I watched in amazement as my grandchildren seemed to have their parents up two or three times a night until they were quite old. Like most babies Andy had his yelling times, usually in the early evening, and there were times when I phoned an SOS to Gwen who would come and calm both of us down.

I owe much of my independence to Mac's attitude towards me. He never fussed around offering to help me but left me to do what I could – and sometimes what I didn't think I could do. At first he would help me in and out of the bath. One evening I asked for his help when he was reading and I kept getting the response, "Just now." Finally I was fed up so tackled the task on my own – and managed. I went though, flushed with success and the effort involved, to be greeted with "At last!" I never again needed his help with bathing.

When Andy was a year old Mac was promoted to become officer in charge of the police in Kafue. This was a small railway town about thirty kilometres south of Chilanga and it was quite rough. In 1963 Zambia was not yet independent and it was a colonial police force so Mac was in charge of members of the local force as well as three assistant inspectors on contract from UK. One of them was married with a family and two were bachelors.

While in Kafue I came to see another side of Africa. There was a police launch on the river and sometimes I was able to go on patrol with Mac, travelling up the river into the flood plain area. There was fantastic bird life and seeing my first pelican in the wild was a great thrill. Along the river banks there were fishermen smoking their catch and the pungent smoke drifted far along the river. They would make fires with green wood and suspend the fish on poles in the smoke in order to preserve them for their own use and also to sell in Lusaka. Mac's love for the country and its people was infectious and I soon shared his enthusiasm and seized every opportunity to go into the bush with him. I particularly enjoyed our fishing expeditions, sitting on the river bank and usually catching black barbel which David and his family enjoyed. If we caught silver barbel I would soak them in milk and cook them for us.

There were many hippo in the river and they had to be approached with caution as they would rear up out of the water and could overturn a boat. When the river was in flood a hippo bit a dug-out canoe in half, killing one of the fishermen. The other one had managed to climb a small thorn tree but the hippo was butting it, trying to dislodge him. This all happened within sight of the bridge so Mac was summoned and had no choice but to shoot the animal in order to save the man. The beast was then butchered on the spot and the meat distributed among his staff. Mac returned triumphantly with a large joint which was so fresh that it was actually twitching! I was not impressed so minced it and made a curry just to be sure it was really dead! Mac and Ted often went hunting or fishing together so it was quite normal for me to have a spurwing goose, duck, guinea- fowl, venison and fish in the deepfreeze. Nothing is tastier than a spurwing goose cooked in beer!

Mac had won a scholarship to go to university in UK and as he had failed, we had to repay the government so money was very short. In the bush, about 15 kilometres from the town, was Kafue Methodist Mission, situated on the river. As well as a clinic there was a secondary boarding school for boys and I went there to teach. Driving to school one morning I saw my first lion in the wild as a lioness strolled across the dirt road in front of my car, real Africa. Teaching at the mission was quite a challenge as I was the first woman on the staff. The boys were suspicious of me at first, however, they quickly got used to me and then I was treated as an expert to answer their questions on sex! They wouldn't ask the male staff as that would show an unacceptable lack of knowledge in their minds.

I had one sobering experience when teaching there. Shortly after I arrived I gave the most senior class a test. These were mainly 'boys' in their early twenties, not much younger than me. Some of them had obviously cheated and, in my ignorance, I told them that only stupid people cheat. Imagine my horror when they all got to their feet and demanded to know how I dared to call them stupid. I was actually quite frightened and shouted at them to sit down, which they did, to my relief. I then explained my reasoning and the lesson ended peacefully. The following morning the headmaster was waiting for me as I drove in to school. He had heard what had happened and told me that it would be better if I didn't teach that class for a while. I disagreed and he reluctantly allowed me to continue. When I finally left the school about a year later those same boys asked if I would agree to shake them each by the hand so that they could say thank you. I was very moved. About eight years after I left the mission I was recording results at the National Inter-schools Athletics competition in Chingola. Suddenly a young school teacher who was there with his team rushed up to me and enthusiastically shook my hand. He had been in that class at the mission and we had a good chat, reminiscing about the old days. He was quite dismayed to hear that I was leaving Zambia.

In 1963 Zambia experienced several minor earthquakes as Lake Kariba had been filled and the bed of the lake was sinking slightly. One of these quakes struck when I was teaching and the boys just fled out of the classroom. I was unable to follow as there was a deep step out of the room. I just sat there giving thanks that there was no glass in the windows, just mosquito gauze, and that the plaster falling from the ceiling came down in flakes, not chunks.

On another occasion I arrived at school in the morning to find the headmaster standing alone in front of the school. As I parked there he came to tell me that the boys were on strike! I had never heard of such a thing. Apparently they had suddenly decided that the food was not good enough. It was a year prior to Zambia's independence and was obviously a politically motivated act. All the boys were dismissed from the school and told they would have to reapply in order to return. Education was really prized in the country at that time and every boy wrote begging to be reaccepted, with the vast majority stating that they had been intimidated into joining the strike. After about ten days school life was back to normal.

One of the staff tasks was to collect school fees at the beginning of the year. Each boy had to pay twenty pounds which covered everything. As the boys were all boarders it included food, uniforms, two blankets and any writing equipment and books that they required. My heart ached as one old man came to my desk and started emptying two shilling pieces out of his pockets, out of a grubby handkerchief and out of his floppy hat. It was exactly the right amount and when I nodded his face was wreathed in smiles as he signed the form with a cross. He was illiterate, as were most of the parents, and hence his joy at being able to educate his son. In the first week of the first term we constantly had to check the class registers as boys would join the classes without being members of the school. On one occasion a boy was being continuously disruptive to the point that I sent him out of the class. After he left a hand went up "Are you a Christian Mrs Thomson?" "Yes". "Then how can you deprive Phiri of his education ?" Such was the value placed on education in those days, sadly it changed when education became available for all.

In the early 1960s the new lake at Kariba was a fisherman's paradise and requisites for fishing expeditions were earthworms for catching bream. Kafue is on the main road to the lake so Mac came up with the idea of breeding earthworms to help our finances. He acquired about ten 44 gallon drums, had them cut in half lengthwise and put them under the mango trees by the police station. They were filled with manure from my in-law's cows to which some soil and kitchen waste was added and then Mac stocked them with Californian Red earthworms.

The worms bred quickly and then my job started. On a Thursday afternoon Mac would bring home some buckets of earthworm mixture and old oil cans. I sat at the dining room table, which I covered with newspaper, and counted out 100 worms for each tin, adding a little of the compost which was almost odourless as it was so well decomposed. The remaining compost was wonderful for the garden. Enock became our salesman. He was an old man who had a small stall on the main road where he sold a few vegetables and tomatoes. We made signs for his stall and on a Friday morning, on my way to school, I would drop off about 25 cans for the weekend trade. He was delighted as he made a profit of sixpence a can and also increased his vegetable sales. It was a win/win situation as the extra cash was a welcome addition to our budget – where there's muck there's money!

Shortly after arriving in Kafue I was again pregnant. This prompted some of the boys to go to the mission clinic and demand to know from the elderly Scottish spinster in charge, how many children she had. When she said "None" they informed her that she had failed as even Mrs Thomson was pregnant! She told me this with much laughter. I actually taught there until I was nearly eight months pregnant.

"Weeping may remain for a night, but rejoicing comes in the morning."

Psalm 30 v 5

L ife at home was quiet as there was little entertainment and no TV. We started inviting the young expatriate policemen to play cards and have a meal with us some evenings and we had many happy times together. My nightmare began one Friday afternoon. Mac came home early, rushed into the house, grabbed his revolver and then roared off on the police motor bike. We had agreed to have the usual crowd for cards that evening so I drove to invite the wife of the married assistant inspector and her husband to join us. She seemed lonely and I had tried to include her in some of my activities. In the course of the conversation I said that something must be on and described Mac rushing home and out again. To my total horror she burst into tears.

"He is going to kill himself!" she sobbed.

"Why ever would he do that?"

"Because I said that I won't marry him ".

Then the whole sordid story poured out. They had been having an affair for about six months.

The bottom dropped out of my world. I had no idea what had been going on and here I was, four and a half months pregnant. I drove back to the house, picked up Andy, and drove to my in-laws' farm just outside Lusaka. My mother-in-law and I were very close and she was as shattered as I.

I still loved Mac and asked him to give our marriage another chance. His mistress had two small children and her husband was not prepared to divorce her. Mac's superior officer in Lusaka heard what had happened and within days they were to be transferred to Livingstone on the Rhodesian border and a few weeks later we were informed that we were transferred to Kalulushi on the Zambian Copperbelt.

At Kafue we had a large run in the garden with spurwing geese, guineafowl and hens. In addition we had two duiker that Mac had rescued as babies from men trying to sell them illegally. Mac decided that we should have a farewell braai (barbeque) and we would slaughter the chickens for the event. He asked Wonder, the gardener, to kill them. A short while later, there was a huge shrieking of terrified hens from the back garden and then Wonder knocked on the kitchen door and asked if he could have Bwana's revolver. Mac went out to discover what was happening only to find all the hens with their legs tied and hanging upside down on the washing line. Wonder was planning to shoot them. However gloomy life may seem there is usually something to make us smile.

Kalulushi was a small mining town and did not have a government hospital, which was why I returned to Llewelyn Hospital for the birth of Jonathon (now known only as Jo). I again had a Caesarean as he was also breach. When the nurse said, "You have a beautiful son," I burst into tears. I was convinced it was a girl and thought that a daughter might make all the difference to my marriage. To my dismay that reaction upset the staff who thought I wouldn't love him but nothing could have been further from the truth. My sons have given me so much joy.

On 24th October 1964 Zambia became an independent country. Mac, being the officer in charge of police at the time, was invited to the independence ceremony and took me with him. It was very moving seeing the Union Jack lowered and then the new Zambian flag raised to the accompaniment of the new national anthem. The chairman of UNIP, the new governing party then gave an address and took us all by surprise when he denounced Sir Roy Welensky as a tractor! We had been given printed copies of his speech and there, sure enough, was the misprint. Presumably it should have read as traitor – was this a sign of the future ?

When Jo was six months old Mac had the usual three months leave and we flew back to UK to be with my parents for Christmas. Once again we sailed back to CapeTown on the *Pendennis Castle*, bringing with us a new car fitted with hand controls. In CapeTown we met up with my mother-in-law and drove up the coast of South Africa, through Rhodesia and back to Lusaka. Mac had been promoted to assistant superintendent and we were posted to Bancroft, later renamed Chililabombwe, on the western end of the Copperbelt, just 16 miles from Chingola.

Money was still a problem and so I again went back to teaching at Chingola High School which was by then a mixed race school. Andy was now four and the Mother Superior of the convent agreed to accept him in the infant's class. Every morning we were up at 6.00 and it was a rush to get him dressed, have breakfast, and then drive to school. He would climb into the back seat of the car and sleep until we arrived about fifteen minutes later. At that stage the school day for me finished at 1.00 so I could pick him up and take him home. Jo meanwhile would still have a morning sleep and when he woke our cook looked after him.

The presence of animals was an integral part of life with Mac. We had a cat and a German shepherd dog but he was always rescuing some wild life. When we arrived at Chililabombwe it was to discover that twenty seven African grey parrots had been seized from smugglers bringing them over the border from Zaire. These birds were at the police station but started to die so Mac began bringing them home for me to nurse. He took one corpse to the vet who found that the birds had fatty livers, probably as a result of being fed nothing but peanuts on their journey from Zaire. In the end we managed to save two birds and, as no one in the police seemed interested in their welfare, we kept one and gave the other to Mac's parents. That bird, Bobby, is still alive and very vocal. He lives with Jimmie and Iris (Mac's brother and wife). Our parrot Mouche died in 1983.

Apart from bush hares which Mac frequently brought home, he also rescued a civet which wandered around the house until it started slinking up on the parrot and then we gave it to a wildlife specialist. There was a young spotted eagle owl which would sit on a pelmet, moaning quietly, provoking furious shrieks from Mouche. As the owl grew up it would fly out at night to hunt, returning to sleep on the pelmet during the day, until one morning it didn't return. At one point we had two bush babies. They are delightful, cuddly animals but also antisocial. They were always awake and active at night and it was almost impossible to keep them contained, so every morning there were hand and footprints around the picture rails. I became disenchanted with them when I discovered that they urinate on their hands in order to hang on more easily!

One morning Mac was called out to a village in the bush. The villagers had dug a deep trench around their gardens to protect their crops from wild animals and a hippo and her calf had fallen into it. Try as they might there was no way to save the mother so Mac had to shoot her. He and the constables with him managed to lift the calf out and brought it back to the police station. Dumdum as the calf was called, was housed in the garage at the police station and Mac constructed a makeshift pond but the next problem was feeding her – my task! Hippo milk is very rich so I mixed milk, baby cereal, eggs and glucose. The mixture was only part of the problem, the next part was how to feed it to her. We tried a baby's bottle – hopeless with that huge mouth, rubber gloves – she just bit through them. Finally we resorted to a hot water bottle and that worked. Feeding her was a full-time job. Every morning we would wake to hear her grunting and calling as our house was next to the police station. At the time our dog, Mwaiche, had just weaned her puppies and Dumdum tried to suckle from her so they began to play together. She was about the size of a large pig and seeing her crouch down with her front legs was very funny. Dumdum's story was published in the newspaper and Mac received an offer for her from Frankfurt zoo but hippo are protected game in Zambia and after a few weeks she was taken away to Lochinvar government game ranch. The last time we saw her was at the agricultural show in Lusaka, which was rather sad.

On November 11th 1965 the whole school was called to assemble in the quad and the headmaster announced that Ian Smith in Rhodesia had made a unilateral declaration of independence. Little did I think that that declaration would have repercussions for me in the future. When I went home that day Mac gave me money to shop for supplies of tinned food and non-perishable goods as the border between Zambia and Rhodesia was to close and we were anticipating difficult times.

Mac's secretary, Linda, was a younger single woman who had drama training and she encouraged me to become involved in the theatre again. As a result I produced a light comedy called *The Tunnel of Love* for the opening of the Bancroft Theatre. Bancroft had a church so I was able to attend on most Sundays and was asked to join the church council which I did. When I reflect on those times I realise how busy I was and wonder whether I was trying to prove something and whether my busy-ness contributed to subsequent events.

Mac had always enjoyed horse riding and at the police training school at Lilayi had often ridden in police escorts. Bancroft had a very active Gymkhana Club so he took advantage of it and bought himself a pony, Roger. From then on most weekends were spent at the club where there were tent-pegging and jumping competitions. In the evening there was often a braai and dancing to taped music. That was where I 'danced' in my wheelchair – great fun but it needs a lot of room to avoid crashing into other couples. Linda seemed to be lonely and had few friends so I suggested to Mac that we invite her to come along with us. Before long she became my closest friend in Bancroft and we included her in most of our activities.

At independence the government policy was to Zambianise the civil service. Mac, being born there, felt that his job in the police was secure but then the policy changed and became Africanisation. That meant that his job was secure but he would never be promoted so he began to consider his options. After much soul searching we bought a cattle and maize farm just outside Lusaka.

I was about to start packing for the move when Mac told me that he wanted a separation and that I should speak to the headmaster about having government accommodation for myself and the children in Chingola. It is said that anyone can make a mistake once but only a fool makes the same mistake twice. I had done the latter, having again befriended a lonely young woman. Linda was moving to the farm with Mac. I should have known better as by then I was aware that he could not resist the opposite sex. I was shattered and felt totally betrayed by someone whom I had considered to be a friend.

*"Carry each other's burdens,
and in this way you will fulfil
the law of Christ."*

Galatians 6 v 2

At first the children and I were accommodated in a ground-floor flat. I couldn't manage to use the single toilet so had a commode in the corner of my bedroom. Not an ideal situation. There was a step outside the door of the flat and therefore I was unable to go out without help as, at two and four, the boys were too small to help me.

My greatest concern was how I could manage to look after Jo and teach. In desperation I visited Mother Superior at the convent and explained my problem. She didn't hesitate, "Jonathon must join Andrew in the infants' class. I know that on a teacher's salary you will struggle so there will be no charge." I tried to demur, although I wasn't sure how I would cope, but she was adamant, "When we are starving we shall come to you for a crust of bread." When I look back I am awed at the way the Lord cared for us.

I wondered how Jo would settle at school as he was just over two. In my mind's eye I can still see this wee boy in his khaki safari suit, which was the school uniform, swinging his minute case and striding out behind his big brother on his first day at school. I of course drove off in tears! Mornings were a huge rush. I had to get the boys dressed and give them breakfast before washing and dressing myself. As we had to be ready to leave the house when my domestic worker arrived at 7.15 there was never time for me to have breakfast. I subsequently discovered how unwise that was as my energy levels slumped mid-morning and I struggled on until lunch time.

In the first school holidays both boys went down with measles, this being before there were MMR injections. Andy had it mildly but Jo was very ill. On the Sunday morning Jo was running a very high temperature and I was desperately worried about him. I didn't have a phone and, because of steps, I couldn't get out of the house to call anyone. Once again the Lord had things under control – why do I ever doubt him? A woman whom I hardly knew came to visit me. She had never been before and I was overwhelmed with relief when she arrived. She called a doctor (they still made home visits in those days) and he diagnosed bronchial pneumonia which he immediately treated.

Shortly after this, single quarters became vacant and I moved. These quarters were semi-detached bungalows with small gardens. There was only a single bedroom but with a screened stoep area leading off it, which was where the boys shared a bed. Not ideal but better than the flat as I could manage the bathroom. In the next school holiday both boys had mumps and in the following holiday they had chicken pox so that was all the main childhood ailments over in a year – but what a year!

The boys were happy at school and I was enjoying my teaching. At that time there were four expatriate English bachelors teaching at the school. They all took me and 'the prodge', as they called the boys, under their wings. Without their help I would have had a real battle and been lonely but they took me shopping and we often went on picnics in the bush, with me driving over dirt roads and rickety bridges as I was the only one with a car. At weekends, if it was very hot, we went to the primary school swimming pool and one of them would pick me up, leaping into the water with me in his arms. Getting out was a little more complicated but somehow they managed it.

I am not sure how it started, but we began the gourmet club on a Monday evening. Charles, Terry, Allan, Dave and I, and later Breda joined us. We always met in my house as I had the children to consider and we took it in turns to cook a continental meal. Those not cooking brought a bottle of wine. I still cook some of those dishes we tried out then. The evening usually finished with their pushing me for a walk around the town.

The bachelors were all younger than me, and I had a more permanent home so they would often pop in for coffee and keep me company, or take me to the Theatre Club. Among our friends were Martin and Marge. They were older than us and Martin was the deputy head of the school. Marge came to me one day and criticised me severely.

"You are neglecting the boys because the bachelors are always there and they never spend time alone with you," she said. I was shattered and defensive – and then began to think. I am everlastingly grateful to Marge for that criticism for she was right. From then on my house was off limits to visitors from about four in the afternoon until the boys were in bed. I still believe that a true friend must be prepared to point out something that he or she believes to be wrong. It is also my belief that none of us like to be criticised but we should look carefully at criticism and decide if it is valid. If it is, act on it, if it isn't, forget about it.

"We are hard pressed on every side, but not crushed; perplexed, but not in despair; persecuted, but not abandoned; struck down, but not destroyed."

2 Corinthians 4 v 8 & 9

Shortly after Christmas 1966 Mac phoned me and asked me to move down to the farm and give our marriage another try. I was more than happy to do so despite any misgivings I had. I still loved him and, in my heart, blamed Linda for what had happened. I also felt that the boys needed their father. I applied to the Ministry of Education for a transfer to Lusaka and was posted to Kabalonga Boys' School to start in the first term 1967. I was thrilled as Seth Bottom was the headmaster and he and Maureen had remained my friends since my pre-accident days in Chingola.

The farm house was typical of the old farms, large and rambling with a screened in stoep (verandah) on three sides. Cooking was on a wood stove in the kitchen and there was a paraffin fridge. Both items were temperamental and inclined to stop working at the most inconvenient times. More trying was the fact that the farm lay in the stink-bug belt. These are ghastly insects which are more accurately called shield beetles because of their shape. They are about a centimetre long and emit a dreadful stench when they bump into anything. During the rainy season they descended in their millions and got into everything. Every morning David, our domestic worker, would sweep out large heaps of them and still they would return. The smell permeated the whole house.

As a sideline Mac had started growing vegetables and flowers. I would drop them off with a market stall holder called Zulu on my way to school, and collect the money and containers on the way home. Some of the staff at school asked me about supplying them with vegetables so I took orders and spent about an hour every evening packing them for the following day. In the evenings I also dispensed basic medicine to the workers, treating diarrhoea, constipation, coughs and colds as well as headaches. On three occasions I had to drive to the hospital in Lusaka with workers who had snake bites. There was never a dull moment.

My days were full as I dropped and collected Andy from primary school. Teaching ended at 1.00 and I was usually back home by about 2.30. We had one Jersey cow that we milked and I made our own butter about once a fortnight. It was a messy job as I didn't have the right equipment but it was worth it. I really enjoyed the farm life.

I also started an adult literacy class in the barn on weekday evenings. Most of the farm workers were illiterate and could not write their names. I acquired books from those running the adult literacy campaign. For the first week I had only our farm workers but then those from neighbouring farms started to arrive and finally I had to restrict numbers. It was an exercise in patience. Communication was in 'Chilapalapa' the lingua franca in Zambia as there were so many languages. There were twelve different languages spoken on our farm alone.

For a couple of months everything seemed to be going well but then Mac started coming in from the lands in the evening, bathing and going to town, only coming home in the early hours. I later discovered that Linda had returned from long leave in UK and the affair was on again. I closed my eyes to what was happening and prayed that it would pass. I felt desperately hurt and helpless and nursed a deep hatred for Linda in my heart as I still blamed her. She had once told me, before I knew about her relationship with Mac, that people could not help falling in love. My response had been to agree but to add that a person could control how they acted on it. I became aware that when I was on my own I would be conducting imaginary conversations with her and was letting hatred consume me so I made a great effort to put her out of my mind, but it was very difficult when Mac went off to town.

On 21st June 1967 my day started as usual, dropping vegetables off at the market, taking Andy to school, teaching, picking Andy up, collecting the vegetable baskets and money and driving home. The road to the farm was a dirt road and had been freshly graded which had left a ridge of sand along the edge. As I drove along there was a tractor in the middle of the road so I hooted and prepared to overtake. The tractor veered to the right so I pulled over, hit the soft sand and had a blow out at the same time. There was nothing I could do to control the car, it rolled and Andy was thrown through the windscreen, as I was later told. I was thrown out and the car rolled over me.

A nightmare again. I kept passing out and in my conscious moments heard Andy crying. I was begging someone to help him. I recovered consciousness again and couldn't hear him and was frantic but a man told me that he had been taken to hospital. An ambulance had been called for me but never arrived so one and a half hours after the accident my mother-in-law arrived and I was put in the back seat of a mini and taken to hospital. All I remember is saying, over and over, "I haven't broken my back, it is already broken."

Andy had been given four pints of blood and rushed into theatre. He had a fractured femur and pelvis and the skin had been taken off the back of his right leg as he went through the windscreen. I was told later that it was a miracle that he survived the blood loss. I was also told that the theatre sister led everyone in prayer before they started operating.

I was in and out of consciousness for about twenty four hours and my blood pressure was apparently dangerously low. After about three days the nurse making my bed noticed that my left foot was at a strange angle and that I had broken my ankle, so I also had surgery. My body was black from the waist down and only a year later, when I went for a check up in Stoke Mandeville, did the X-rays show that I had a fractured pelvis and femur. The head of the femur was in the pelvis socket but the shaft was free and because it was never set my left thigh is now shorter than the right.

As soon as I was allowed out of bed I went and stayed with Andy in the children's ward for most of the day. He was recovering well but had to have a series of skin grafts, so was in and out of theatre. A nerve had been nicked in his pelvis and he had no sensation in his foot. He was incredibly brave and positive throughout and the nurses were so impressed by this five-year-old. I was just devastated to see him having to endure all the trauma.

When I finally went home Jo also returned as he had been staying with Jimmie and Iris in Kabwe. It was wonderful to see him again. Things with Mac had not changed. Just to complicate matters further there was a petrol shortage and I could visit Andy only once a week. There was no vehicle that I could drive so I was driven in the bakkie by Wilson, our tractor driver. It was heartbreaking when I had to leave after visiting Andy as all I could hear was this voice crying, "Mummy, I want to tell you something." The final crunch was that I developed a deep vein thrombosis so was prescribed anticoagulants and had to have my blood tested daily. There was no petrol available for me to do this so Seth and Maureen said that Jo and I should stay with them in their house at the school which also meant that I could visit Andy in hospital more frequently.

While I was there Seth and Maureen both had a serious talk to me and pointed out that the life I was living was not fair on either the boys or myself. I was so unhappy that I was only really being half a mother and for the first time I began to seriously think about divorce. The thought terrified me. Not only did I love Mac but I could not imagine how I would cope with the boys on my own, as a disabled person and on a teacher's salary. I knew that Mac would not have the money to pay me any maintenance.

At last my blood stabilised and I was told that it would need only weekly testing so Jo and I returned to the farm. More petrol became available so I was able to return to school, still driven by Wilson. It was good to be home but it did not change the situation with Mac.

Finally Andy was discharged from hospital but the surgeon advised that we arrange to send him to England to have the plate removed from his femur and to have more skin grafts. My parents agreed that he could stay with them in Weston-super-Mare and they would arrange for him to go into the children's hospital in Bristol for the surgery. Marianne, my sister-in-law, was planning to look for a job in UK so in November 1967 she and Andy flew over from Lusaka airport. It was such a wrench to see them go and Jo was a very sad little boy.

On a Saturday morning, shortly after Andy left, Mac again asked for a divorce and threatened to take the children from me if I would not agree. It was obvious that this was the end of the line for my marriage. How I wept. I think I must have cried all day. In retrospect I realise that I was crying for the three great losses in my life. The rejection by my father when I said I would marry Mac, the loss of my physical independence when I broke my back and finally the break up of my marriage. I felt as though my heart was broken. Looking back, I thank God that he had his hand on me and gave me the strength to come through.

I started divorce proceedings. Mac now spent every night in town, arriving home just in time for Wilson to drive me to school. At this time the bush war was being waged in Rhodesia and our neighbouring farm was a training camp for freedom fighters, terrorists, as we called them then. They were members of Joshua Nkomo's ZANU army and our workers always told us when a group had moved out to mount an attack in Rhodesia. The soldiers were armed and started to come at night to shoot and steal our cattle for food. As often as not the phones weren't working and, even if they were, the police were not anxious to take any action. I felt very vulnerable as Jo and I were alone in the house.

On one occasion, late in the evening, there was much shouting and hammering at the back door. When I opened it there were six of our workers, all drunk, almost carrying, Lucky, another worker, who had been seriously stabbed. I had no vehicle and the phone was not working so all I could do was bandage him up as best I could. Not an easy task, with me sitting in a wheelchair trying to treat him, and calm down the drunken crowd that was increasing in size by the minute. The following morning, when Mac returned, he discovered that there had been a fight and my patient had come off most lightly. The other man, Enoch, had his eye almost gouged out and had run off into the bush.

Meanwhile Andy had been operated on to have the plate removed from his femur but his foot which had lost sensation had dropped and he had been fitted with a calliper. He was back with my parents and they had arranged for him to attend the local primary school and he wrote asking me when he could come home. I didn't tell my parents anything about my situation and the divorce as I knew that my father would have a very emotional response and I didn't feel I could cope with it.

Divorce proceedings were set for the 10th June at the High Court in Lusaka. Marianne, my sister-in-law had returned to Zambia and had booked a flight to UK on the 12th for Jo and me. After endless visits to the Ministry of Education I was posted back to Chingola High School for the August term and was promised a house. Packing up my belongings was a soul-destroying job.

I think many people who have gone through a divorce would agree that it leaves a sense of failure. I also found it hard that, as the innocent party, I was the one who had to appear in court and talk about my husband's adultery. I tended to blame it on my disability at the time but I know now that paraplegics can have happy and successful marriages. Mac simply could not cope with what had happened to me although, in his own way, I believe he loved me to the end. I kept asking the Lord, "Why?" and felt at the time that my prayers were not being answered but now I know that He brought good out of what happened. Only later did I come to acknowledge that it takes two to make and two to break a marriage and I was not totally blameless. I realise, in hindsight, that I tended to over-compensate for my disability by being constantly busy so couldn't have been a very relaxing person to be around. Years later Mac told me that one of his problems with me was that I wouldn't have a row with him! That was true. As an only child I didn't have siblings with whom to have rows and I certainly would never dare argue with my parents. To this day I will always avoid confrontations whenever possible.

Mac drove us to Lusaka Airport and as an attendant was pushing me through he called Jo back and gave him a final hug. When Jo caught up with me he said, "Daddy says to tell you he loves you." It took all my self control not to sob.

Our arrival in England at Gatwick was quite traumatic. As an air hostess took charge of Jo he shouted out in amazement from the top of the steps,

"Mummy, look at all those white people!" His two-year-old treble caused many heads to turn. I was then lifted onto a small chair with four little wheels and pushed out onto a platform facing the airport building where friends and relatives were lined up to greet passengers. The man helping me moved away and the chair tipped over backwards. There I was in my smart new suit with my skirt over my head and my legs up over my shoulders. Fortunately I wasn't near the edge of the platform. I rarely wear trousers as they are difficult to put on, but from that day on I have always worn them for flying.

CHAPTER **9**

"He gives strength to the weary and increases the power of the weak."

Isaiah 40 v 29

It was wonderful to be with Andy again and for several days he wouldn't let me out of his sight but our stay was also very stressful. When I told my parents that I was divorced my father's reaction was twofold. First that it was what he had always expected and secondly that we wouldn't tell anyone. This was 1968 and divorce was still regarded as shameful. He stated firmly that if I loved the boys I would return to England permanently. I explained that in Zambia I could have domestic help just like anyone else there, would teach in the mornings only, for the most part, which would give me more time for the boys, and finally the climate suited me as cold weather gave me chilblains on my legs because of the bad circulation. All these were true reasons but I also knew that if I returned to UK he would try to control my life and I didn't feel capable of coping with that.

After two months the boys and I flew back to Zambia where we all had to adapt to life in a one-parent family. The government supplied me with a brand-new three-bedroom house in Kabundi, a suburb of Chingola. I could manage the loo as there was a bathroom, washbasin and toilet combined and that was a huge relief. There were steps to get out of the house but I had ramps made for the front door and stoep, they were too steep for me to manage alone but with the boys' combined help we could cope.

On both the previous occasions that I had lived in Chingola I had experienced the ferocious thunder storms that occur, mainly in the rainy season. I was told that in some way copper attracts them although I was never fully convinced of that. Shortly after moving into our house there was quite the worst storm that I had ever known. It happened in the middle of the night and woke us up with the crashing of the thunder and the howling wind. We were all understandably nervous. As I was trying to keep the boys calm I saw, in the lightning, that a tall tree in the back garden had just snapped and twisted around as though held by a giant hand and just prayed that nothing would come through the roof. The following morning revealed a scene of devastation and as we drove to school there were trees down all over the roads. I learned later that many of my neighbours had parts of their roofs ripped off so we had escaped relatively lightly. An event like that made me feel very vulnerable and somehow being disabled seemed to heighten that sense of vulnerability.

Andy was now six and started at the government primary school. He still had a calliper which he had to wear day and night and for about two hours daily I had to supervise his exercises and also massage the scars with lanolin cream. He wore the calliper for a year in all and it did the trick. Now, at 47, he still tends to walk on his toes on one foot but the injury hasn't interfered with his playing sport at school and university. When time allows he still enjoys playing squash and going water skiing.

Jo returned to the convent and was warmly greeted by the nuns. Chingola High School had now changed its name and become Chingola Secondary School. This was the third time I had taught there and I had seen it change from an all-white to a 90% black school. The staff was multiracial including several Indians who were there on contract, as well as some new expatriates from UK. Martin and Marge were still there, Martin now being the deputy head. As always they were wonderful to me. My salary did not come through for two months and I was desperate but they helped me out. It was not unusual for Martin to arrive on my doorstep with a delicious curry, claiming that he had cooked too much for themselves. As ever the Lord blessed me with wonderful friends. Charles, one of the gourmet club bachelors, was now back in England and lent me money to buy a car. Terry, another of the bachelors, and Pete, the priest on the staff, drove it up from Durban for me.

The boys had great freedom where we lived. They played with their African friends in the bush near the house and had impromptu picnics there. Opposite the house was a huge anthill, about six metres high. One of their favourite games was sliding down on their bottoms which had serious repercussions on their shorts so I tried to encourage the use of cardboard to sit on, with limited success.

There were new buildings going up at the end of our road and on one occasion Jo came rushing in to me in deep distress.

"Mummy, Andy is stuck in the new church building and can't get out."

"Well how did he get in?" was my question.

"He climbed through the window."

"Then he will have to climb out again," I replied and, as Jo ran off with my instruction, I sat there agonising about what I could do. Needless to say Andy did get out on his own. I think it was incidents like that which made the boys very independent. They knew I was unable to run to their assistance if they were climbing trees and the like, so had to be sensible. At the same time they were boys and I couldn't wrap them in cotton wool.

I am not sure how it started but it became routine that friends gathered in my garden for a braai on Sunday evenings. Everyone brought their own meat and drinks and the boys and I enjoyed the company. One evening that sticks in my mind is when we were looking at the moon and saying, "Can you believe that there is a man up there ?" The following day there was a headline in the Times of Zambia, 'Ndola policeman doubts American Claim' – it went on to say that this cop had been watching the moon through binoculars and hadn't seen the landing!

I still enjoyed my teaching but some of the extramural activities, with which I was called upon to help, were a bit tricky. I was detailed to run the agricultural club which was no hardship as I have always been interested in gardening. We developed a good vegetable garden but sadly much of the produce vanished during the school holidays. My greatest challenge was to supervise rugby practice. Not only did I know nothing about rugby but this female in a wheelchair trying to rush up and down the touch line caused much mirth. Fortunately I was soon relieved of the task. One of my roles was to discipline the pupils who were late for school. This involved being armed with a blackboard ruler which I had to apply to the backsides of boys and the hands of girls if they were late. It was a job I did not enjoy and I usually lent a sympathetic ear to excuses like "The bus died" or "I came footing."

One activity that I thoroughly enjoyed was assisting the French teacher in producing Shakespeare's *Julius Caesar*. The majority of the cast consisted of Zambians and my task was to help with the pronunciation of the main actors. The whole production was great fun and the crowd scenes were spectacular. Casius was played by a Sikh pupil who donned a white turban for the performances as being more fitting with his white sheet toga than the usual maroon.

Chinese influence was now becoming obvious in the country. The Zambians at school began wearing badges with Chairman Mao's effigy on them and many proudly brandished the *Little Red Book* of his sayings. I wrote to the Chinese Embassy in my role as a geography teacher and requested any information on the country that might be available. From then on I received a monthly magazine entitled China Reconstructs. The Indians on our staff were very alarmed and asked how I dared to read it. In fact I found the rhetoric very amusing – the toothless dog of America etc. Madam Mao was involved in Chinese culture at the time and there was a full account on the new opera *How we took Tiger Hill by Force*. Apparently she had called for military topics in theatre. In 1970 China began the construction of the TanZam railway (now called Tazara railway) linking Zambia with Dar-es-Salaam.

I was really struggling financially at this stage and the boys were aware of it. When Jo lost a tooth and the tooth fairy came in the night and put five ngwee under his pillow he came through to me and proudly announced, " Mum, when all my teeth drop out we will be rich and you won't have to worry." Shortly afterwards I drove home from school one afternoon and saw two small boys sitting by the side of the road with a basket and a toy blackboard saying, "Lemons 5 ngwee each."

"What ever are you doing?" I asked in horror.

"We found all these lemons in the kitchen so we thought we would sell them and make some money," was the response.

"Has anyone bought any?"

"Oh yes, Jim up the road bought five."

My humiliation was complete – it was Jim up the road who had given me the lemons in the first place! Fortunately he and his wife thought it was hilarious.

One thing that the boys inherited from Mac was a love of animals and before long we had quite a menagerie apart from the dog, cat and parrot. Paul our domestic worker/gardener helped build a run in the garden and the animals accumulated and bred. Some were given to the boys by my in-laws in Lusaka and others by friends and included rabbits, guineapigs, tortoises, bantams and ducks. From time to time there would be a commotion outside with dogs barking and, as I couldn't get down the step from the kitchen, Andy would go out armed with a torch and accompanied by Mwezi, our dog, to see what was happening. With my being disabled the boys took on more responsibility while still young, than would be normal in most homes.

Mac came to visit from time to time but all too often he opted out at the last minute, leaving two very disappointed little boys, and me making excuses for him. I vowed that I would never speak against their father to the boys and I never did. I find it hard to understand divorced parents who have nothing good to say about their 'ex' as the children have genes from both parents. When Mac and Linda were married I explained that Daddy didn't love Mummy any more. The next time Mac did visit he was very cross because Andy had greeted him with, "Why don't you love Mummy any more?" He wanted to know why I had told them that when it wasn't true! Human emotions are so complex.

Forty years on I look back on some happy times there, like the 10-kilometre sponsored walk in which I was persuaded to take part! A broom handle was tied across the back of my chair and I was pushed by Lazarus (black) Stuart (white) and Josie (coloured) We had a hilarious time. Inevitably I had a puncture just before the end but somehow a bicycle pump was obtained and we made it back. Our arrival was recorded as 'The first group to return pushing a wheelchair!' Needless to say we were the only group with a wheelchair.

In 1969 I was called into the headmaster's office and informed that I was to have lodgers. As I was in government accommodation I had no say in the matter. The stores department arrived at the house with bunk beds for the boys which just fitted into the tiny spare room and the lodgers had their old room. They turned out to be a red-headed Yorkshireman called Ian, and Edvige, his petite French wife, who spoke English with a Yorkshire accent. They were good company but I must confess to being relieved when, after about six months, a flat was found for them as planning meals on top of all the other activities was quite a strain.

When I first returned to Chingola Martin and Gwen, who were Jehovah's Witnesses, opened their hearts and their home to me. They were incredibly kind and generous, taking the boys and me camping on Lake Bangweulu and on holiday to Malawi, where we stayed in a hotel on the lake and returned via the Luangwa Game Reserve. The Bangweulu trip was a real adventure as we camped right by the lake with Martin helping me down onto a camp bed. The boys went out with some fishermen in a dug-out canoe and just loved it. We spent a couple of nights there and imagine our horror when we were packing to leave and someone came along and told us that a child had been taken by a crocodile on the beach where we were camped !

Inevitably Martin and Gwen spoke to me about their faith and invited me to go and worship with them. For a couple of weeks their beliefs were tempting because everything was clear-cut and no personal decisions seemed necessary. At a time when I was sad and weary of making major decisions I was very vulnerable. When I look back now I can see the Lord's hand in my life then, as I came to the realisation that their faith was not based on the Bible as I understood it. I also became aware that I had allowed my grief over the divorce to dominate me and had neglected my spiritual life so we started going to Church again. Martin, Gwen and I remained friends but things were never quite the same and it is a sadness to me that when I left Zambia we drifted apart.

My teaching contract was due to expire in 1972 and, as education standards in Zambia were declining, I began to contemplate our future. In

1970 my mother's youngest sister came for a holiday and I planned a trip around Rhodesia. We had a wonderful holiday visiting the Victoria Falls, Wankie Game Park, the Matopos, Zimbabwe Ruins and on to the Eastern Highlands. At this last destination we stayed in Umtali and visited the Drapers who had been so kind to my parents in Kitwe after my accident. When I mentioned the possibility of returning to England Dick Draper was horrified and took me to meet the newly retired headmaster of Umtali Boys' High School who convinced me to apply to teach in Rhodesia. I applied and was offered a job at Umtali Girls' High School.

CHAPTER 10

*" For I am the Lord, your God,
who takes hold of your right hand
and says to you, Do not fear;
I will help you. "*

Isaiah 41 v 13

On 1st May 1972 the boys and I drove over Christmas Pass and saw Umtali below us, nestling in the valley. We were tired and the little station wagon was loaded with Mwezi, our very large dog, Cassidy, an African grey parrot in his cage, and a pile of luggage. Jo has always told me that when we first saw the town I said, "I wonder whether we will ever learn to call this place home." Certainly I didn't think I would spend the major part of my life there. Once again I was moving to a new country where I knew only two people but now the boys were with me. They were only ten and eight but were great company and also very helpful, if only at picking things up that I had dropped, and taking care of the animals.

The Drapers were wonderful and we stayed with them until I was able to sort out my house. As I was working for the government I was given temporary accommodation for the first six months until I could find somewhere of my own. Unlike in Zambia, where furniture was provided, I now had to start from scratch and Dick took me around to make my purchases. Wherever we went the person serving asked, "Are you new in town ?"

" Are you going to work here?" "Where?"

As soon as I said I was starting at the Girls' High School the response was " Oh, you're with Drac!" The headmistress was universally known as Dracula. I could never have imagined then that, years later, I would give the eulogy at her funeral!

The school was almost in the centre of the town but with large grounds. It had originally been a co-ed school and, as it catered for boarders, it served most of the Province of Manicaland. It increased so much in size that a new school was built for the boys on the outskirts of the town and girls remained in the original buildings. When I arrived the school was already about seventy years old and there were still horns of various animals such as buffalo and kudu mounted over many of the doorways. The older buildings were single storey with corrugated iron roofs which reverberated as though there was an earthquake when the vervet monkeys thundered across them. Torrential rain was deafening and hail could almost bring lessons to a halt.

My first year was very difficult. Not only was Drac a hard taskmaster, but I was also house-hunting. If I looked at one I must have looked at 50 houses. The centre of the town is in the valley but the suburbs are on the slopes so finding somewhere without either steps into the house or a split-level garden was a real mission. Once again the Drapers gave me good advice on areas to avoid and finally it was Dick who took me to see the house that I finally purchased. It had a wide central passage and large rooms so that manoeuvring around the house in my chair was easy.

On 11th November 1972 we moved. I had a fridge, stove, beds, two armchairs and a dining room table. When I had put the boys to bed that night I just sat and cried, wondering how I would ever get organised. Slowly, however, I did get the house furnished, mainly with second-hand furniture from the local mart. The house had parquet flooring which was a real blessing as carpets were not necessary. Carpets and wheelchairs do not go well together as the wheels do not run freely and, when staying in carpeted homes, I find pushing my chair very tiring.

Our new house was old by Rhodesian standards, having been built in the 1940s. It was all on the level and had a large stoep where we always had breakfast and lunch. The stand was an acre and a quarter so there was a large garden area with a variety of fruit trees including peaches, oranges, lemons, bananas, mulberries and avocados. Over the years I added pawpaws, lychees, naartjies (tangerines) and mangoes. There was also a large vegetable garden so I employed a full-time gardener. He and my domestic worker stayed in the double quarters on the property and had their own area of garden with banana and pawpaw trees and room to grow their mealies (maize) and vegetables. The rose garden gave me great pleasure. There was a large variety and the previous owners of the house left me a plan showing the names of the 50 types so, once we were settled, I entered specimens in the Umtali Flower Show. I was thrilled to win the rose bowl twice. It was a huge embossed silver bowl resting on three kneeling elephants – a real labour to clean !

When I bought the house the previous owners had left eight hens in a sizeable run and with a good solid hen house so fowls became a feature of our life there. One day a bantam hen suddenly appeared in the garden and moved in and she hatched many batches of fertile eggs for us. It is amazing to think that I sold eggs to friends at 25 cents a dozen, now, in January 2008, a dozen cost Z$ 13 million which is two million less than the average teacher earns. The only problem with the hens was that they attracted various predators. On one occasion a serval managed to get into the run and just bit the heads off the hens without eating them – what a waste! The eggs were periodically stolen by rats, snakes and a pair of mongooses which moved into the garden from time to time. It was an ongoing exercise to keep all this wildlife out of the run.

I had received a gratuity from the Zambian government which I put down on the bond and then added the cost of putting in a swimming pool to the bond. The pool was about eight metres long and was built with a ramp starting at the height of the seat of my wheelchair. In order to get in I wheeled up to the ramp, lifted my legs onto a small flat area at the top of the ramp, pushed my footplates back, moved forward until the seat was level with the ramp and then slid into the water. Getting out just meant doing the whole thing in reverse. It was always a rush before going to school in the morning but I swam twenty lengths at 6.20 throughout the summer. Now that I have retired I have more time to put to it and swim 500 metres every day – arms only of course. Not only is swimming good for my general health but it also helps me to keep my weight under control. I can gain weight very easily, being sedentary, so am very careful about what I eat, except when on holiday. Lifting in and out of the car, into bed, onto the toilet etc, involves carrying weight on my arms and shoulders and they do not need extra strain.

Once we were settled the boys and I joined St John's, the Anglican Church and I joined a house group run by Chris and Helga. The first time I attended I was startled by the singing of choruses and open prayer, all completely new to me, nevertheless I continued attending and came to a completely new understanding of what it meant to be a Christian. In my previous experience the Holy Spirit was rarely mentioned and neither was having a personal relationship with Jesus, it was a complete revelation to me and from that time my faith has been all-important in my life. I become very irritated by those who write 'religion' off as a crutch for the weak. Being a Christian involves self-discipline, not an easy way out. From that time I got up early every morning to have a quiet time of prayer and bible reading, and church became immensely meaningful for me. I know with complete certainty that I could not have coped with all that has happened without the Lord's help. It is my constant prayer that my family may come to know Christian joy.

From the time we arrived in Rhodesia, when the boys were eight and ten years old, I made a point of going on weekend expeditions. I bought a map of the area and the three of us explored the highways and byways. The boys had worked out how to lift my chair out of the car by a combined effort. One of our favourite outings was to Lake Alexander which supplied Umtali's water. I would sit on the shore while they swam or, when they were older, went out in a rowing boat. Happy days.

We soon entered into the activities in the town. The boys joined the swimming and judo clubs and took part in training and competitions. Not only was I 'Mum's taxi' but I also became involved, particularly in the swimming club. I spent many hours sitting by the Olympic size pool recording results. Both boys were Cubs but Jo was really keen and went on to become a Queen's Scout and attended a Jamboree in Switzerland. I also trained as a Samaritan and spent three hours manning the phone at the

Samaritan office every Tuesday afternoon. We didn't receive a lot of calls so it was a chance to catch up on letter writing.

One of my first friends in Umtali was Tony. He was a confirmed bachelor, a few years older than me, and he took the boys and me under his wing. Umtali was about five kilometres from the Mozambique border and at least twice a month Tony would arrive saying, "Let's go abroad." We would drive over the border either to the station at Machipanda or to the swimming pool at Vila de Manica and gorge ourselves on seafood, mainly prawns, crab or oysters, washed down with Portuguese vinho or Cervejas (beer). The meal inevitably ended with crème caramel and my mind always goes back to those days when I see it on the menu. The Rhodesian dollar was very strong so these were always cheap outings.

In 1975 Mozambique became independent under the Frelimo government. We continued to visit for a while but things began to change. On our last visit we watched barefoot boys aged about twelve or thirteen wearing scruffy khaki uniforms and carrying AK 47 rifles, which was quite alarming, and then in March 1976 the border was closed.

1956 – Elspeth and I in typical pose, she is talking while I listen!

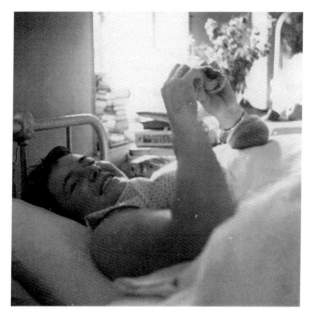

May 1960 – Stoke Mandeville; attempting to make a teddy bear.

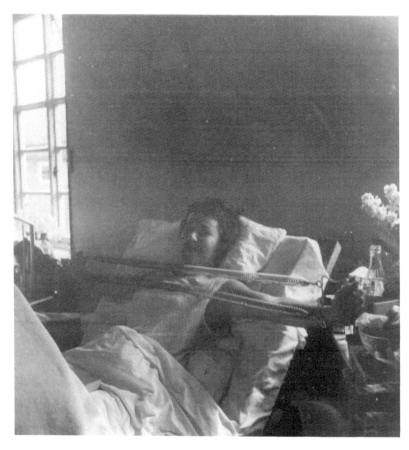

May 1960 – Stoke Mandeville; Tarzan in the making.

August 1960 – Stoke Mandeville; out of doors at last.

April 22nd 1961 – Joyful day.

1962 – A proud mother.

1967 – Andy analysing   Jo tucking in

1982 Table Mountain, Cape Town – Wine in hand

1983 Eastern Cape, South Africa – Hard on the chair but great fun.

1987 University of Cape Town – Andy's graduation with my proud parents, Jo and I.

2004 Mutare, Zimbabwe – With Faustina; preparing to swim (socks and all).

2006 Hoedspruit, South Africa – Taking to the air.

2010 Knysna, South Africa – A trip in the family boat

December 2010 Knysna, South Africa – With all my family at their holiday home.

CHAPTER 11

" The Lord is my rock, my fortress and my deliverer; my God is my rock, in whom I take refuge. "

Psalm 18 v 2

When we arrived in Rhodesia I was largely unaware of the political situation in the country and everything was infinitely better than in Zambia. Not only were there more goods in the shops but health and education facilities were excellent. Trade sanctions imposed by the rest of the world were circumvented to some extent, and what couldn't be imported was manufactured in the country using a high degree of initiative and ingenuity. At that time the country was second only to South Africa in industrial development in the whole of Africa.

Shortly after we arrived men began to be called up for regular periods of army service, sometimes as much as a fortnight in every six weeks. Meanwhile boys leaving school were enlisted for two years of national service. The seriousness of the situation really came home to us in August 1976.

Early that month the boys and I drove to Salisbury (Harare) to collect my uncle, aunt and cousin Cathy from the airport, as they were coming to stay for three weeks. We were very excited at the opportunity to show them around. We had just gone to bed on their very first night when there were huge explosions fairly nearby. My uncle, who had fought in the Second World War, took it very calmly and said it sounded like mortars. On the following morning it turned out that there had been a mortar attack launched from the ridge overlooking the city. Fortunately they were Russian-made mortars and the majority did not explode as they had not been properly primed. The boys rushed out early and went to the golf course nearby, collecting an assortment of tailfins and shrapnel. One house had been hit in the attack but no one was injured.

Now everyone was on high alert. All the windows in the school had tape stuck across them creating a diamond pattern in order to protect against flying glass. The schoolchildren in the city had to have their names clearly painted on their school cases so that anything unidentified could be brought to the attention of the bomb disposal squad. We had a system of whistles at the school. One whistle meant everyone under their desks, two meant evacuate the building. I was teaching one morning when suddenly all the girls dived under their desks leaving me looking bewildered. It transpired that they had heard the games mistress blowing her whistle in the gym!

Now we were really at war. It was forcibly brought home to us when family members of close friends were killed. JeanAnn was the first person to befriend me at school and she and her husband Trevor were wonderful to the boys and me. Their eldest son, Tony, was killed just before he was due to be demobbed prior to going to university. Such a dreadful waste of a young life. In one attack four men from Umtali were killed by a direct mortar hit while they were on duty. A few years later Betty, the widow of one of those men, became my very close Christian friend and mentor.

Two women blew themselves up while attempting to assemble a bomb in the changing rooms at one of the biggest stores in town and as a result we were all subjected to searches when entering shops. Volunteers visited all the houses to identify the safest location in which to shelter in the event of more mortar attacks. I had a room under the house where we stored garden implements, the boys' bikes, chicken food, etc. This, I was assured, was the safest spot so I had a ramp made for the steps in case we had to use the bolt hole. I was only two when the Second World War broke out and we were living in Newton Abbot in Devon. It was an important rail junction and therefore a target for the Germans. I remember my father carrying me down to 'under the stairs' when there were air raids. This was little more than a large cupboard where brooms, carpet sweepers and other items were stored in peace time. As most houses in Rhodesia were bungalows there were few such safe areas.

The big difference between World War II and the Bush War was that the latter was a guerrilla war and, similar to today's terrorist attacks, it was necessary to be on the alert at all times. Having said that, I have a vivid memory of playing in the rock pools at one of the south Devon seaside resorts when my father came running, "Come on Margaret, quickly!" He picked me up and ran up the beach with me in his arms to where everyone was crowded below the beach wall. Flying in low from the sea were planes which began to strafe the beach. Even then I recognised the high-pitched whine of German planes and associated them with danger. Any fear I felt was heightened by a woman nearby who was screaming and crying. I had never seen an adult cry before and her terror stayed with me for a long time, which is probably why I remember it all so clearly.

In fact Umtali experienced three more mortar attacks. One occurred in the late afternoon when the boys and I were at the municipal pool with the swimming club so we sheltered there. The other two were at night so the boys, Lydia, my domestic worker, the gardener and his family, our two dogs and I all huddled in the storeroom. We prayed together and listened to the local radio station to find out what was happening. The last attack was the most frightening as the mortars were obviously landing nearby. The morning after we discovered that one of the fir trees in our garden had been beheaded and one wall of the house had been chipped by shrapnel. After each attack the boys couldn't wait to get to the golf course on their way to school to see what trophies they could find.

Many of our pupils were boarders whose parents were farming and landmines planted on farm roads were a major hazard. Two of our girls suffered landmine attacks, one being killed and the other losing both legs. When the latter returned to school in her wheelchair a couple of cement ramps were made to facilitate her movement between the buildings which was a bonus for me as I no longer had to travel the long garden route around the grounds to reach the staff room. As the war escalated more and more people had friends or family who had been killed or injured.

The stress of the war really hit me one afternoon when the boys and I were in the garden and a Dakota plane lumbered overhead towards Mozambique. For no apparent reason I burst into tears. Quite a few people were leaving the country and I wondered whether I should do the same. When I mentioned this to the boys Jo immediately said, "You have often told people that you believe the Lord brought us here, why do you think he would speak in a whisper if he wanted us to leave?" Out of the mouths of babes and sucklings! I didn't question our presence again.

In April 1977 the boys and I were invited to join some friends for a fortnight on the Wild Coast in South Africa. It was quite a journey. There were convoys organised on all the main roads. Each convoy was accompanied by armoured vehicles and on occasion helicopters flew overhead. The convoy speed was 90 kph so journeys took longer than normal and were more exhausting as one had to keep a watchful eye on the vehicle in front whilst ensuring that there was no wide gap. In all we had to join three different convoys before reaching the South African border but the holiday by the sea was well worth the hassle.

We were in a self-catering flat from which we crossed the road onto the beach. Every day the boys pushed me down on to the sand, not easy. We have often discussed the option of a sedan chair for such journeys. Once there they helped me down to sit on a towel on the sand so that I could read while they swam and generally explored. On occasions like that I was very thankful for my tough skin as I did not have a worry about pressure sores as long as I took the weight off my tail from time to time. When our friends arrived Tom would carry me into the tidal pool so that I could swim which was such a joy for me.

On our way home we had been invited to spend a few days with friends on their sugar estate in Chiredzi. We had no sooner left the convoy to travel through the bush to the farm than we had a puncture. Now what? This was a hot area for attacks and there was no one in sight. I could do nothing but Andy and Jo leapt out of the car and changed the wheel with the speed that would have impressed those at a Formula One pit stop.

In the Vumba mountains, about 15 kilometres from the town, there was a private preparatory boarding school catering for boys from throughout

Rhodesia and from Zambia. As the situation worsened the school closed down and the buildings were taken over by the Elim Mission school as it seemed more secure than the original location further away in the mountains. It was there that one of the most dreadful atrocities of the war occurred. One evening in June 1978 the mission was attacked and eight British missionaries with their four young children were killed. As though that were not enough, the women and small girls had been raped – the country reeled with shock.

In spite of all these tragedies our daily life continued its routine with the three of us deeply involved in school activities. Both boys played hockey and water polo for the school and frequently we were up before 5.00 on a Saturday so that I could drive them to school to catch the bus to Harare at 5.30. Harare schools were not keen to travel to us because of the possibility of mortar attacks.

It was when they were taking part in a judo competition and staying overnight in Harare that I had a rather alarming incident. Just after lunch on the Saturday an army Land Rover came up the drive and out climbed a very tall, broad, black soldier with a large plaster on his face and carrying an FN rifle. He introduced himself as a friend of Tony's and said that Tony had recommended that he visit me if he was in the area. His next statement took my breath away. "I am desperately in need of money as I have some trouble with the army. Please, can you help me?" I began to feel anxious and assured him that I had no money in the house whereupon he showed me a document from the army saying that he was charged with murdering a fellow soldier. I was so shocked that I didn't think to question how he came to be travelling around the country if that was the case. He asked to make a phone call back to his barracks in Harare which he did, and then asked if he could return later, but I said I was going out, which was not true, but by then I was feeling very apprehensive.

After he left I phoned my neighbours and told them what had happened and we arranged that I should call them if he returned. At about 7.00pm the phone rang and it was him. He spoke first and, on the spur of the moment, I replied in a very deep voice saying,   " Maggie is out and I have come to stay!" Whereupon he put the phone down. About half an hour later a vehicle that sounded like a Land Rover drove to the front gate but I had put on a lot of lights in the house and it drove off.

The drama continued the next day when I received a visit from some white army officers demanding to know my relationship with this man. I explained exactly what had happened and they told me that they had traced the call he had made from my house as he had stolen an army Land Rover, grenades and rifles and gone AWOL (absent without leave) as he was facing a murder charge. They gave me a phone number to ring if he tried to contact me again but, thankfully, I heard no more. I felt very vulnerable and was so glad when the boys came home. I never did hear the end of the story but Tony told me later that the military police visited him as well.

"Lord, you have assigned me my portion and my cup; you have made my lot secure. The boundary lines have fallen for me in pleasant places; surely I have a delightful inheritance."

Psalm 16 v 5 & 6

In 1979 the Lancaster House agreement was signed in London and an interim government headed by Bishop Muzorewa was put in place with the country renamed Zimbabwe Rhodesia. This was followed by the first free election in the country with all adults entitled to vote. It was in that election that Robert Mugabe was first voted into power and the country became known as Zimbabwe.

In August of that year Mac invited us all to go and stay with him at Kariba. He and Linda had divorced so we were just our family together again. He had his own boat which he kept at the lake and we had wonderful times. My greatest thrill was to catch a six-kilogram tiger fish from the boat. It really fought and it was so strong that it threatened to pull me out of my seat so Jo held onto me. The next thing was that the reel parted company with the rod and Andy tried to hold it in place while Mac was armed with the keep net. I am still not sure who was most excited by my success, the family or me!

Bringing up two boys as a single mother isn't easy for anyone but the strict discipline in their schools helped enormously and also the fact that they are so different. Andy is always the academic and rather more introverted. He did well at school, was awarded academic colours, and graduated in medicine without a hiccup. Jo, on the other hand, is an extrovert and born leader so it was no surprise that he was head boy at both junior and high school and head student of his hall of residence at university. He was always so busy organising something or other that his studies had low priority so I heaved a sigh of relief when he graduated. I am sure it is because they are different that they are the best of friends.

One thing they do have in common is their father's wicked sense of humour. I was swimming one morning when they came rushing out shouting, "Snake! Mum! Snake!" Sure enough there was a snake swimming towards me. I raced to the ramp – as fast as arms only would allow – and then realised that they were laughing. It was a snake alright, but it was their harmless house snake that they had thrown in to join me!

National Service for 18-year-old boys was scrapped to my great relief. Andy would have been conscripted when he finished school in 1980 but was now free to go straight to university. As a young child he had always wanted to be a vet, but when he was about 13 he suddenly decided that he would like to study medicine so in February 1981 he set off for the University of Cape Town. That was the end of an era. He came home for vacations but now it was just Jo and me.

Shortly after Andy left, Lydia, my domestic worker, told me she had found a factory job in town and would leave at the end of the month. I knew she wasn't very happy as I wouldn't allow her boyfriends to stay on the property so it wasn't a complete surprise, but finding a trustworthy replacement could be a problem. 'Oh ye of little faith.' The Lord had it all in hand. Friends were emigrating to South Africa and their domestic worker, Faustina needed a job. For the next 23 years she became my housekeeper and my friend. We had our ups and downs as was inevitable with two women in such close contact but she was a committed Christian and she taught me a lot. She had three daughters who finally came to live with her. They were accepted into the high school when they were old enough and used to travel there with me.

I employed a number of gardeners over the years but one who became a family legend was Lazarus. He was mentally very slow but very hard-working and had green fingers, everything he planted grew. He also often frequented the hospital at weekends with some imagined ailment. His claim to fame was due to 'the case of the surgeon's cap'. When Andy came home one vac, he turned out a variety of old clothes which he gave to Lazarus. Inadvertently he included a green surgeon's cap that he wore in theatre during his medical training. One Sunday I received a frantic call from Lazarus at the police station, "Please come and help me, I have been arrested for wearing the doctor's hat!" There followed a garbled conversation with him in tears. It had been raining that morning so Lazarus had donned the offending cap and gone to the hospital where he was instantly apprehended by a security guard and accused of stealing it from theatre. The police were called and his protestations of innocence fell on deaf ears. I explained to the cop on duty what had happened, was severely reprimanded for allowing him to wear the hat and was allowed to rescue him from the police station. Two days later a police Land Rover arrived with four policemen who came into the house to return the cap and give me another lecture. I tore the offending item in two in front of them and told them that it was now a duster. Interestingly, their visit was at a time when anyone reporting a burglary was invariably told that the police couldn't come because of 'no transport!'

Enid and Frank came to stay in 1982 and it was wonderful to catch up with Enid and reminisce about our days together in Stoke Mandeville. I have always driven a station wagon as it is easier for getting the wheelchair in and out and, at that time, it meant that we could load both chairs. Jo and I drove them up to Kariba where we stayed with Ted and Gwen, our friends from Zambian days, while they went by air to Wankie Game Reserve and the Victoria Falls.

All too soon Jo also left for university in Cape Town and I was on my own. I am very much a people person and don't cope well with loneliness so when both Andy and Jo suggested that I take in a lodger, it seemed a good idea. It meant that I was able to pay Faustina more so she was also happy. Over the next twenty or so years various people lodged with me and most have remained friends – Ketil from Norway, David from England and Murdo from Zimbabwe, to name but a few.

It was a few years after the boys left home that Di, a very good friend, suggested I learn to play bridge. I didn't feel I had time but she insisted and made up a table with herself as teacher and two friends and colleagues, Ann and Kathleen. I have owed her a huge debt of gratitude at her insistence as, not only do I enjoy my bridge, but it has introduced me to people who have become friends.

I had many visitors to stay and it gave me great pleasure to show them the beauty of the Eastern Highlands. Elspeth, my closest school friend, and Derek, her husband, came and were able to play golf at different courses including Leopard's Rock in the Vumba Mountains which was then world famous. There were my university friends, Selma and Meg, with whom I had shared a flat. Selma and Jack came over from Australia and Meg and Brian from England. Hugh and Lindsay, my Cornish cousins drove with me to South Africa as did two of their daughters, Bridget and Jackie. The girls each came with their boyfriends/husbands on more than one occasion. There were many others and, being an only child, these visits by friends and relatives were particularly special for me. I still become very excited at the prospect of visitors.

"That everyone may eat and drink and find satisfaction in all his toil – that is the gift of God."

Ecclesiastes 3 v 12

Throughout my teaching career I felt it was important not to expect special consideration for my disability and consequently tended to overcompensate by volunteering for everything. I am sure this is a characteristic of many disabled people. Early in my life as a paraplegic a so-called friend told me that my problem was that I had never accepted the fact that I was a second-class citizen. She was right, I have never been prepared to be considered as such. It isn't what happens to you but how you handle it that is important. I detest the word invalid. Because one is disabled in some way, does not make one 'in valid.'

I was teaching Geography and one piece of equipment that made my life easier was a blackboard that could be rolled up and down so that I could draw maps. Towards the end of my career an overhead projector became available which was a luxury as I could prepare maps and diagrams ahead of lessons. Not only have I enjoyed teaching but it has been a God-given career for someone in my position. Apart from anything else I was able to be at home when the boys had their holidays and my working day was similar in length to theirs.

Once the boys left home, school became the centre of my life. Following Independence the composition of the school changed and from being all-white it became multiracial and by the time I retired it was about 98% black. Staff were expected to take part in extramural activities and for several years I taught swimming and was also the adult advisor for Scripture Union. In the late 1980s the presence of AIDS began to make itself felt in Zimbabwe and Dr Foster established the Family AIDS Counselling Trust (FACT) in Mutare.

It was under the auspices of FACT that I started an Anti-AIDS club in the school. The aim was to increase AIDS awareness which we did by having talks, debates and producing plays. The club was the first of its kind in the country and as a result we had visitors from other schools and also from other African countries, especially Kenya, Uganda and Zambia. Now the majority, if not all, of Zimbabwean government schools have similar clubs.

The problem is exacerbated by poverty. When girls grow up without any little luxuries and a 'sugar daddy' comes along offering them some cheap trinket in exchange for sex, they are often tempted. One of my pupils told me quite frankly that if it was a choice between earning money for her schooling and taking a chance on AIDS she would choose the latter.

AIDS also affected me domestically. My gardener, John, had not been well for a long time and was losing weight so I was reasonably sure that he was HIV- positive. He came to me in great distress to say that his baby boy was sick and he subsequently died in the local hospital. John was at a loss to know what to do so Faustina advised me about how I could help. In the end I negotiated for the coffin and, with my car packed with John, his wife, Faustina and various relatives, went and collected the body from the mortuary. I transported them all to the cemetery with red cloths attached to the wing mirrors of the car to indicate that it was a funeral party. I had taken my wheelchair out of the back of the car to accommodate the coffin and was quite relieved as it meant that I couldn't attend the funeral where I would have been out of place among the loudly grieving mourners.

About a year later John asked me whether his wife could come and stay on the property as she was sick and needed to go to the hospital. She normally lived with the children in their rural home. For the next fortnight

I spent a lot of time taking her for treatment, being woken at midnight on one occasion to go to the hospital. There were no anti-retrovirals at that time and the hospital would not admit her as they were overburdened with AIDS patients. John decided that she must see the witch doctor who said that she must go back to her village to appease the spirits. I agreed to take them the following day but, when I returned from school at lunchtime, she had died. I phoned the police so that they could transport her body to the morgue – only to be told that I must do it as they had no fuel for a vehicle. It took all my powers of persuasion to convince them that I could not do that so they came about four hours later.

Shortly after his wife's death John said that he wanted to give up work and go home. He died a few months later, leaving two more in the ever-swelling number of orphans in Zimbabwe. Scarcely a week passed at school without a message on the staff notice board saying that one of girls had lost a parent.

Teaching in a girls' school opened my eyes to some of the problems they face. I was surprised to discover how many of them came from broken families and what difficulties the girls then had to face. If they lived with their father he invariably remarried and the new wife often used her step-daughters as unpaid domestic workers to the extent that some had only a few hours sleep and no time for homework. If, on the other hand, they lived with their mother, her new husband would frequently abuse them sexually which exacerbated the AIDS problem. Females in African society can have a very hard life.

I enjoyed teaching and was appointed as head of the geography department. My greatest stimulation came from teaching the sixth form and taking them out on field trips. Even during the war we went to do river studies in the bush, with me pushing myself up and down the banks shouting advice while the girls paddled around in gum boots checking the velocity, shape of the river bed, etc. Another favourite trip was to a local granite kopje (hill) where the girls climbed to the top, observing and recording the weathering processes along the way. I sat at the bottom praying that there wouldn't be any problems as they climbed. One particular group stood at the top of the granite cliff waving to me and then lined up and sang the school song which I found very moving. African voices harmonizing are so special. The girls were always very considerate towards me and when I arrived at school in the mornings there would be a couple of volunteers to take out my chair and carry my books.

Without Andy and Jo around I became aware how much I had come to depend on them to help me in various ways at home. My feet always tended to swell so one of the boys would put them up on cushions on a stool if I was watching TV in the evenings. Most of the time I could manage by myself but when I couldn't I learnt to move a foot off the side of the footplate, loop a long scarf around it and lift it like that. Necessity being the mother of invention. Obviously some things are more difficult to manage in a wheelchair but there are often ways and means that can be found to get around the problems.

On one occasion Shadow, our German shepherd, woke me at about midnight, desperate to go out. I let her out but then she wouldn't come back. There was thunder and lightning as a storm approached and then I heard a yelp. Now I was really anxious as I had visions of her tangling with a snake. I couldn't get down to the front gate where I had heard her so the only option was to get in the car and drive down which was what I did. When I approached the gate there was Shadow playing with a huge cane rat that she had killed. I managed to persuade her to get in the car and back to the house where I saw the cause of her yelp. The cane rat hadn't given up without a fight and she had a gash on her nose.

In the early 1990s I began to be very disillusioned with the situation at school as there was a lack of dedicated leadership and a whiff of corruption at higher levels. The whole situation changed in 1995 when a new headmaster, Mr Kwari, was appointed and, for me, it became the most productive and enjoyable period of my career.

If I had to think of one word to describe Mr Kwari it would be integrity, not a characteristic of which many can boast in today's world. He was also a workaholic, with the interests of the school and the girls as his first priority after his family. After the boys left home I had the same priority and as a result we became firm friends. We were also united in our concern for the school leadership. I was elected by the staff to become prefects' patron and in that role he and I worked closely together compiling leadership training programmes for the sixth form. He dealt with the academic side whilst I devised exercises to drive the lessons home. It was very challenging and I thoroughly enjoyed our training days and watching the girls develop their leadership skills.

The prefects would come to me, as their patron, with any disciplinary difficulties they encountered in the school and often with their own personal problems so I came to know them well. One very emotional event occurred at speech day a few years before I left. The head girl was making her farewell speech and got as far as, "I want to thank Mrs Thomson" when she began to sob and couldn't continue. After a couple of minutes she started again but once more burst into tears at the same point. The deputy head girl then stepped into the breach, taking up the copy of the speech, but also broke down when she reached the point of thanking me. Finally Mr Kwari took over. It was a very moving occasion for me as I knew the girls considered me to be very strict but we also had a great rapport.

Under Mr Kwari's guidance the school regained its former good name for its excellent results and the general quality of the pupils. The staff could once again feel proud of their association with it.

I also have reason to be grateful to the head for introducing me to computers. I still feel that my computer has a mind of its own but I would be lost without it. The Internet has also opened up a new avenue of communication. Many of my old pupils have kept in touch and they are spread all over the world. One of my old boys whom I taught in Zambia even tracked me down, no longer a boy but now a man in his 50s.

Very recently I received a request on Skype to be linked with someone whose Skype name I didn't recognise. I agreed to link up only to hear a female voice say, "Do you remember me? You taught me geography." It transpired that she was speaking from China where she is teaching English as a second language. As her first language is Shona I am full of admiration. Just over a year ago Charné registered me on Face Book which has resulted in even more contacts. It is said that a teacher's influence extends to eternity,

I don't know about that but, judging from the messages I receive, it does extend world wide.

I am immensely proud of our 'old girls'. Some have gone on to become doctors or lawyers, not only in Africa but also in developed countries like UK, USA and Australia. Their achievements are so varied. Others are mothers, occupied in what is arguably the most important career of all – bringing up children.

"Always giving thanks to God the Father for everything, in the name of our Lord Jesus Christ."

Ephesians 5 v 20

Every November, for over 20 years, my parents came to stay for three months and in latter years my aunt came with them. Andy and Jo came home for their long vac. so we were together for Christmas which was lovely. Every Sunday we would have a braai and all had our tasks. Andy would make the fire, Jo did the braaing, Mum made salad, Dad dispensed beer and I prepared the meat and rolls. After lunch my father would lie on a lounger by the pool, heave a contented sigh and say, "I pity all those people in England now where it is freezing and miserable!" They all really enjoyed wintering in Africa and my father was a great help in keeping the house in good repair. He last painted the outside of the house when he was well over 70, recruiting the gardener to paint the chimney which involved climbing over the roof!

With both boys now at university in Cape Town I began to visit them in the April school holidays. It was quite a complicated journey. On the last day of term, school ended at 10.30 so I went straight home to change and the drove 2½ hours to Harare. A quick stop with Joan and Roy and then to the airport from where Joan drove my car home and kept it there. The worst part of the journey was being taken onto the plane in Harare. There was no special transport for the disabled so I was put on a narrow chair, similar to the one on which I had come to grief at Gatwick, and was then carried up the steps onto the plane and lifted into a seat. Quite nerve racking. In Joburg I had to change planes but at least there was modern transport for the disabled and elderly.

Those visits to Cape Town were very special. I stayed with friends from Zambian days and the boys spent their spare time with me. Mac had bought each of them a car when they went to university so transport wasn't a problem. We had wonderful days out on the wine routes, travelling along the coast and also going up Table Mountain in the cable car. It is such a beautiful area, the only drawback is the weather. Capetonians always say that they have four seasons in a day and they are not far wrong. Since being disabled I feel the cold very badly, probably due to the poor circulation in my legs. Incredible as it seems, I was living in the tropics but had chilblains on my feet and the backs of my legs every winter.

On one of my visits the three of us drove in Jo's car, named Amanda, to Luderitz, on the coast of the Namib Desert. The scenery was amazing and I was thrilled to see the different types of sand dunes, about which I taught. On our second day we decided to travel along the coast on the sandy track which served as a road. When we reached our destination, a deserted bay, Jo decided to drive off the track and closer to the sea. As we approached the shore the wheels started spinning and the car became firmly entrenched. Now what? We were about 30 kilometres from the town and hadn't seen another vehicle or building on our journey. Our supplies consisted of three beers! I was off-loaded to lighten the car while the boys hunted for stones to pack under the wheels. Finally, after over an hour of battling in the heat, Amanda was on the move again to our intense relief. Such events make holidays memorable.

In December 1993 my parents didn't come for their annual visit as my mother had broken her hip and had a replacement but wasn't up to travelling, so my aunt came on her own. She and I were preparing to drive down to visit the family in South Africa when my father phoned to say that Mum had collapsed the previous night and had died that morning. My aunt was 84 and father was adamant that we should not fly back for the funeral but continue with our trip. One problem about being a paraplegic is that planning is necessary when making a journey and with all my relatives being elderly I knew that I would be a liability. As it was both Andy and Jo flew over to support their grandfather.

From then until 2000 my father and aunt continued the annual visits and every year I drove them down to South Africa to spend time with the family. I really looked forward to their visits and it was always a busy time with entertaining as they had made many friends in Mutare over the years.

The weather in Mutare is generally fairly predictable, warm during the day, even in winter, and cool at night. Although there is occasional drizzle, 'guti' in winter, it lies in the summer-rainfall zone. In February 2000 there was a major weather event as the city was hit by cyclone Eline. My father and aunt were staying with me at the time and when it hit around midnight we were all up. The hurricane-force winds howled around the house and as we looked into the front garden the three huge pine trees along the front fence keeled over into the road one by one. It brought home to me the sense behind planting deep-rooted indigenous trees as the shallow pine roots were just ripped out of the ground. The rain came down in torrents and soon the whole garden appeared to be under water as far as we could see, and then the power failed. There was nothing we could do so we all went back to bed, although I am sure none of us slept.

The following morning I managed to get out of the drive after John, the gardener, had removed fallen branches. The fir trees were blocking half the road and as I drove to school it was an obstacle course of fallen trees and pools of rain water. When I returned at lunch time my father, at nearly 93, was out in the road busy directing John in the chopping up and removal of the trees. For weeks afterwards the whole city rang with the loud hum of power saws.

Around this time an armed gang was operating in Mutare, burgling white-owned houses and stealing mainly electrical goods. Many of my friends had been targeted and two families who were close friends had been physically attacked and wound up in hospital. When my father and aunt returned to England, two days after the cyclone, I felt very vulnerable as the front wall and fence had been totally destroyed by the fir trees and it was about six weeks before it could be rebuilt. I was a sitting duck in every sense and am sure the Lord protected me.

When Andy and Jo left for university I warned them not to think of getting married before they graduated. About two years before he finished Andy met and fell in love with Gillie who was a nurse. She had been born and brought up in Zimbabwe and her parents were both teachers. In December 1987 my parents, my aunt, and I flew to Cape Town for Andy's graduation and their wedding a week later. Jo was Andy's best man and we had a wonderful family fortnight together. Andy still had his housemanship to do and Gillie was doing her midwifery course so they moved into a flat in Cape Town.

Jo, meanwhile, was due to graduate the following year but missed the ceremony as he and a group of friends went backpacking around Europe and had an amazing holiday. He then moved to Middelburg, east of Johannesburg, and started work in the human resources department of Middelburg Steel. Now my Easter holiday was split between there and Cape Town. He lived in several different flats and I became much more independent about managing the toilet without the aid of a chain such as I used at home. He would be at work all day so I did various household chores and read a lot then at weekends we made trips around the eastern highland areas.

On my very first visit to Middelburg I met Gerrianne who came and asked me to help her with some knitting. She is Dutch and her parents had moved to South Africa when she was a year old. Two years later she and Jo were married in Middelburg and Andy was Jo's best man. I applied for leave and drove down for the wedding with some Mutare friends. One problem when driving in the rural areas of Zimbabwe is the number of cattle, goats and donkeys which wander along the roads. As we drove down on that occasion I came around a corner to find three donkeys strung out across the road. I could not brake in time so had to do some swift manoeuvring in order to miss them. The gap was not wide enough and the wing mirror of my car slapped one on the rump. The donkey merely shook itself and trotted off into the bush while we collected the broken pieces of mirror. That was a minor hiccup on what was a very happy occasion.

From being an only child myself, my family now expanded and it was an immense joy to me when my grandchildren were born. Andy and Gillie first had Claire in 1989. She is now attending an advertising college in Cape Town where she is specialising in graphic art. Then Donavon arrived 17 months later and is at the University of Cape Town majoring in information technology, and playing rugby. He tells me he is now strong enough to take over from Andy in lifting and carrying me!

Jo and Gerrianne have Charné, born in 1993, and Michael, born three years later. They are both doing very well at school. Michael, like his father before him, has just been appointed as head boy for his junior school. I am immensely proud of my family and my grandchildren keep me on my toes. I would be wealthy if paid by the hour for all the games of Snakes and Ladders and Monopoly that I have played! In return they are all helpful in fetching, carrying and pushing for me and I really enjoy their company. They are also very good about keeping in touch and usually I have a chat with at least one of them almost every week which is very heart warming.

Andy and Gillie invited me to spend several holidays with them and the children in Europe and we had some wonderful times. All our holidays were rather hit or miss as far as facilities for wheelchairs were concerned. I always travelled with Horace, an inflatable bedpan, so we could manage if the loo was inaccessible where we were staying. With both Andy and Gillie in the medical profession, they took all the difficulties in their stride.

Our first holiday was in Greece and there I appreciated Andy's strength more than ever. In Athens he hauled me up the glassy marble steps to the Acropolis which was amazing. We also spent time in Crete and Mykanos and it was in the latter that I had my greatest thrill. We all went down onto the beach and Andy carried me into the sea. I had never ever thought that I would swim in the Mediterranean again. It was calm and warm so I swam far out and was quite surprised when Andy came out to me. He said that a Greek family on the beach was very anxious and the father had come to Andy and said, "Your mother, she go!" so he thought he had better put their minds at rest.

On one occasion we spent a few days in Paris which was very special for me. From the age of thirteen to eighteen I had been on exchange visits to France in order to improve my French. For six years I spent six weeks in April/May staying in, or just outside, Paris. On my first trip I stayed with a family who lived on the Isle St Louis with their flat overlooking the back of Notre Dame Cathedral. That was in 1950 and I was allowed to explore Paris on my own while my exchange friend, Florence, was at school. Subsequently I stayed with a family in Nanterre just outside Paris and again travelled in on the Metro to explore on my own. Once I was disabled I never dreamt that I would have the opportunity to return.

The travel agent had booked us into a hotel that supposedly had facilities for the disabled. When we signed in our rooms were on the first floor but there was a lift. The difficulty arose when the lift was too small for the chair. The only solution was for Andy to get in the lift with me in his arms and Gillie would pull the wheelchair up the winding staircase and meet us at the top. It all sounded fine except that I inadvertently pressed the button for the basement! By the time we arrived on our floor Andy was really stressed as I am not a small person. There was some slight compensation in that we were able to queue jump to enter the Louvre because I was disabled. It was wonderful to revisit the places I had seen so long ago.

On all our holidays we spent time with my father, visiting relatives in Cornwall and meeting up with old friends. As a child I had often stayed at Caduscott, my cousins' farm in Cornwall, and I really enjoyed showing the family some of my special places. They also sampled genuine Cornish pasties and now Donavon begs me to make them whenever he comes to stay. We also travelled up to Scotland and through Wales and had wonderful times together. So much for thinking that I should have had daughters – my sons have taken me up mountains, down into caves and into the sea. For them there has been nowhere that I can't go and they always make a plan.

On our last visit to my father we stayed in the house and packed up a lot of his belongings as he had been told by the doctor that he must no longer live alone so he had moved into a residential home. He had a comfortable room overlooking the sea front in Weston-super-Mare but he hated it. We tried to cheer him up on his birthday and Gillie put 94 candles on his cake. They promptly melted and formed a pool of wax on top of the icing! We said goodbye to him in April 2001 and he died in his sleep in September. We mourned our loss but, having seen him in the home, knew it was a release for him. He had a long and productive life and had all his mental faculties to the end which was what he wanted. I could not attend his funeral as I was recovering from my last shoulder operation. So it has been that I have been unable to attend the funerals of those closest to me.

It was a great sadness to me when Andy and Gillie divorced, the day before his 40th birthday in February 2002. He has custody of the children. Subsequently he has become engaged to Sonja and they live in Cape Town.

"Be merciful to me, Lord, for I am faint; O Lord, heal me, for my bones are in agony."

Psalm 6 v 2

In 1983 my parents bought me a ticket to fly to UK and spend my long leave with them. I hadn't had a check-up for years so my father also made an appointment for me to go to Stoke Mandeville in early August and he drove me up. The check-up involved, amongst other tests, a series of X-rays of my spine. The radiographer X-rayed my neck but then did a second series. He told me that he couldn't believe the first ones so did the second set just to be sure. It transpired that there were problems with discs and bony growths in my neck, all of which explained the pain and headaches that I had been experiencing.

To cut a long story short, it was arranged that I have the operation at Southmead Hospital in Bristol at the beginning of September. A trip to spend a week with my cousins on the farm in Cornwall had already been arranged for the end of August and we decided that it should go ahead. We were packed and ready to go when I received a phone call from Jean Ann in Zimbabwe to tell me that Mac had died. I was devastated. In my heart I had always hoped that one day we would get back together. I was able to speak to Andy and Jo which was a blessing. They arranged to go to Zambia for the funeral although they were both suffering from glandular fever at the time.

Acting as pall bearers must have been agonising for them as they loved their father.

Subsequently I have had another neck operation and three shoulder ops. The first shoulder operation was performed in St Anne's Hospital in Harare. I really dreaded it as so many people had told me what a painful operation it is. On the morning of the operation I was lying in bed when I had an incredibly clear picture of myself lying on the bottom of a rowing boat on what seemed to be a lake. As I lay there the waves were becoming rough and there were no oars in the boat. I then sensed a voice saying, "You can do nothing to help yourself now, you have to rely on me." I am essentially a very practical person and not given to mysticism but that experience was so real that I have never forgotten it and am sure that the Lord spoke to me. When I came around from the operation I had minimal pain and didn't need pain killers.

My problems have always tended to be mechanical due to wear and tear on my upper body through lifting myself around. Andy, ever the doctor, says "If we had known before what we know now, you would have lived differently and taken more care of your shoulders." I disagree. I have had a very good and very active life. The only thing that I would have changed would have been to shower instead of bath. Having a bench in the shower involves no more effort than managing the loo but lifting out of a bath is a strain on shoulders. For the past seven years I have also used a transfer board for sliding in and out of the car but that is only because my shoulders really need care.

I remember Dr Guttmann telling us in Stoke that paraplegics should not have electric wheelchairs as we need to keep our arms strong by pushing our chairs manually. I finally got one at the age of 64, on the advice of the orthopaedic surgeon who performed my last shoulder procedure, and it has made a huge difference to my life. I use it only at home so still push myself when I am out but it is a joy to be able to carry things in my free hand. It is also less tiring when travelling up slopes or on grass. In retrospect I should have bought one about four years earlier.

When I had each of my shoulder ops I was totally immobile for six weeks afterwards as I was unable to push myself with only one hand. I needed my food cut up and a lot of assistance with the shower, toilet and bed – all very frustrating. Such dependence is something I still find hard to accept. The one thing I could do was use the computer for e-mails but letters were lower case throughout as I was using only one hand. Altogether I had three operations in Harare when I was far from my family, but my friends and pupils, were wonderfully supportive. Faustina was a loving, caring helper when I returned home and would have made a marvellous nurse.

In January 2001 Hugh and Lindsay, my Cornish cousins, came to stay and we drove to Andy and family in Nelspruit. Andy had bought a share in a game farm on the edge of the Kruger National Park and we spent several days there. Every morning and evening we went out for drives in the game-viewing vehicle and saw a huge variety of wildlife. I always sat in the front seat. On one occasion we had a longer drive than usual and when we returned I discovered that I had serious burns on the soles of both feet in spite of the fact that I was wearing shoes. Only then did we realise that the exhaust passed close under the floor where I was sitting. Any person with feeling in their feet would have been aware of the heat but of course I felt nothing. With help those burns were dressed for several months but in the end I had to have skin grafts.

I have generally been able to avoid any serious injuries although I frequently bang my toes. Recently I had an accident with a pot of boiling tea and burnt my thigh quite badly but it healed quickly and it was one of the occasions when I was glad that I couldn't feel it!

When I had my last shoulder operation in Pretoria in June 2001, I stayed with Andy, Gillie and the children to recuperate. On that occasion I had an 'aeroplane' splint. It was a ghastly contraption which kept my upper arm elevated sideways at a right angle to my body and the forearm forwards at a right angle. I had to wear it day and night for six weeks. The house was very big so Andy left his cellphone with me in the event of my needing him in the night. At that stage I didn't understand too much about cellphones so he showed me which button to press. About two o'clock one morning I was in such agony that I tried to call Andy but pressed the wrong button. What now? I was really at my wits' end. The only number that I could remember was Jo's land line in Cape Town so I rang there! Jo answered and, to his credit, reacted as though it was the most normal thing to receive a call in the middle of the night from the other end of the country, asking him to alert someone in the same house as the caller! Thank goodness for modern technology.

The recovery period from that operation was one of the lowest points in my life. Not only was I in a lot of pain but I felt totally helpless and a burden on the family. Let me say that the feeling was in my mind and not based on the way they cared for me. Gillie particularly was wonderfully supportive in the use of her nursing skills, nevertheless I used to pray that the Lord would take me because I could see no future in my life. At that time I could not envisage ever teaching again let alone driving my car. God has been so patient with me and when I look back I am ashamed at my lack of faith.

Due to the long recovery period from this operation I overstayed my permitted time in South Africa and was ordered to present myself at the Ministry of Home Affairs. Andy managed to load me in my chair into the back of his ambulance to take me to the Ministry. In order to be allowed to stay I had to pay R2000 which would be returned to me when I departed, and also had to be fingerprinted. All went well with fingerprinting my right hand but the left was encased in my aeroplane splint which caused great dismay. Finally the officer taking the prints suggested taking the right hand again but on the left hand sheet - and then discovered that the prints were the wrong way around. In desperation he finally told us to go and I heard no more about it.

When I returned from my last shoulder operation I soon felt fit to teach but was unable to get into or out of my car. Talking this over with friends someone came up with a brilliant idea. I lived quite near to an old-age home where they had a Kombi fitted in such a way that they could transport people in wheelchairs. I phoned and spoke to the lady in charge and for the whole term I was transported to and fro in their vehicle. They wouldn't accept payment so in the end I settled on a donation.

*"God is our refuge and our strength,
an ever-present help in trouble."*

Psalm 46 v 1

In April 2000 I was once again in England with Andy and family and we were staying in Cornwall when Robert Mugabe, the President of Zimbabwe, empowered the so-called war veterans to attack white-owned farms. In theory the exercise was to hand the land over to impoverished peasant farmers but in fact the vast majority of the farms were taken over by cabinet ministers and the like. Many of the war veterans, Wovets as they became known, were far too young to have fought in the independence war. The news in UK was very alarming and my uncle asked me seriously to consider not returning to the country. It was a scary thought. Never to return to my home, friends or school? I couldn't do that and decided that I must go back to Zimbabwe.

The year 2000 really marked the beginning of the serious decline in Zimbabwe's economy. As goods became in short supply, so prices soared and queues started to become the order of the day. Petrol supplies were a major issue and we learnt to queue with bottles of water and something to eat as the queues were so long and movement so slow. Even after queuing there was no guarantee of success as supplies often ran out before one reached the pumps. Cans were banned but people were very clever and had extra tanks fitted inside the boot of their cars to overcome the ban.

In 2002 I managed to fill some cans with petrol so that I could visit the family In South Africa. About a week prior to my departure I was woken by Sheba barking furiously at the back door. When I opened it she rushed out in hot pursuit of someone running down the drive to the front gate. He had a head start and escaped. Faustina heard the commotion and came up to the house only to find that all my fuel hidden in the workshop had been stolen. I couldn't report it to the police as I should not have had it in the first place and anyhow they would not have followed it up. My gardener was almost certainly involved as no one else would have known the fuel was there but I could not dismiss him without concrete evidence. I was devastated as I thought I would have to abort my trip but my friends rallied around and topped up my tank which took me over the South African border where I could fill up.

The days of entertaining friends with three or four-course meals were now over. Not only were ingredients in short supply but the prices were astronomical and way beyond our budgets. Where there's a will there is a way. A group of about 20 of us began meeting at different houses once a month for lunch, and combined our resources. Two or three would provide starters, others the main course and so on. Everyone brought what they wanted to drink and in this way we had some festive parties.

The number of people leaving Zimbabwe increased steadily. Not only the white community but also Asians and black Zimbabweans. The majority of my pupils completing sixth form applied for universities in South Africa, UK, USA and even Australia. When they left it wasn't with the idea of returning when they qualified. There has now been a huge brain drain as more and more qualified people have moved on to greener pastures. Those who left would send money back to their families and it was that money which kept the economy afloat. The majority of the whites left in the country are economic prisoners as they have no external funds and cannot take any money out. If they are pensioners the huge rate of inflation has rendered many of them destitute. Pensioners who had emigrated before the financial crisis also found themselves without their pensions as there was no foreign exchange available, so they were dependent on family members or on charity. I have not received my pension since leaving the country and doubt that I will ever see it.

In the next few years I drove down to South Africa twice a year. The journey to Andy in Nelspruit was 1100 kilometres so I broke it at a motel in Zimbabwe. I always had to arrange to have a passenger because if I had a puncture or any car problems I was helpless. My passenger also went into customs and immigration at the borders to hand in the paper work which I always completed in advance. I usually split my holiday between Nelspruit and Cape Town. Both families had downstairs bathrooms built onto their houses so that I could be independent and I have had, and still have, many lovely holidays with them. I am eternally grateful for the loving care and consideration my family has shown me.

On one occasion Faustina came with me and it was a whole new experience for her. That return journey was the scariest drive of my life. I can no longer drive safely after dark as I have become night blind and as we crossed the border, there was a massive thunder storm. Not only did it suddenly become dark but the rain also came down in torrents. I had to crawl along with Faustina sitting forward and saying "more to the side" or "more to the middle." There were huge trucks racing past us throwing up fountains of water and with horns blaring. I couldn't pull onto the verge as I knew there was at least a 10 centimetre drop from the edge of the tar. I firmly believe that the Lord had something that he still wanted us both to do which was why we made the journey unscathed. It really was a miracle.

After contemplating the possibility of having to leave my home in a hurry I began to ferry some of my more precious belongings down to the family on each trip. On the return journey I brought back groceries and items that were no longer available in Zim. – exciting things like pot scourers!

2002 was a difficult year. Faustina became ill and was diagnosed with kidney cancer. She had the kidney removed at the local hospital and after the operation I received a phone call saying that one of her daughters was to go to the hospital, collect the kidney and take it to the pathology laboratory in the centre of town. I took Janet, her youngest daughter, and we collected the kidney in an unsealed plastic bag – incredible. Following the operation Faustina had to travel to Harare for radiotherapy. The first time she went the nurses said she had to have chemotherapy although this was not what the local doctor had requested. In order to receive the treatment she had to buy the medication herself from the pharmacy. Fortunately I had given her enough money. The chemo made her desperately sick and the nurses were so uncaring that she was very reluctant to go for the second treatment. On her second visit the staff claimed that she had not left the necessary medication with them so she had to purchase more and when she returned home she told me in no uncertain terms that she would not go again. It is a sad fact that in Africa those who rise to positions of authority are often insensitive and very unkind to their own people.

In April 2002 it was my 65th birthday and I received a letter from the Ministry of Education saying that I had to retire. In the past a teacher could opt to continue until 70 but the rules had changed. Encouraged by Mr Kwari I applied to continue until the end of the year, as I was teaching exam classes, and my application was accepted. When it came to the end of the year the parents asked me to continue and the parents', committee paid me for the following year.

The situation in Zimbabwe was deteriorating rapidly. When the commercial farms were seized the farm workers were also chased away which, more often than not, left the land in the hands of those who knew nothing about farming and it became desolate. The economic situation caused many small businesses to close and unemployment rose to over 80%. Food became scarce and prices were prohibitive. Many of our pupils were surviving on one meal a day and some now walked long distances to school as their parents could not afford the bus fares. I concentrated on growing fruit and vegetables to feed Faustina, Isaac the gardener, and myself with any surplus being given to friends. I still kept hens so had a secure supply of eggs as long as layers mash was available.

The roads in the urban areas were breaking up very badly and the idea of filling the potholes with gravel only succeeded in increasing their size. It was said that one should never run over cat's eyes in the road as it could be a giraffe in a pothole! Another joke that went the rounds was that if someone was driving straight you should take care as the driver must be drunk. The rest of us had to swerve constantly to avoid the holes. A joke always surfaced however bad the situation. Nevertheless life had become very difficult.

An increasing problem was cash. There was a shortage and the banks started buying it from the supermarkets, crediting their accounts with 10% over the face value of the cash they collected. Certain notes became unobtainable. On more than one occasion I went to buy chicken food with a large plastic bag full of twenty dollar notes. The joke began to go the rounds that; 'once we went shopping with our cash in our pockets and goods in plastic bags but now the cash is in bags and goods in our pockets!' Coins were still used although one cent pieces had more or less vanished. By 2008 coins were museum items and a 100-billion dollar note had been issued which would just about buy a loaf of bread – if it was available. By 2010 the currency was US dollars or South African rand and inflation declined.

When I went to spend Christmas in Cape Town in 2003, the family persuaded me that the time had really come for me to leave Zimbabwe. They were worried about the deteriorating security and medical facilities. The police could no longer be relied upon to come to your aid in the case of a break-in. So many of the thieves moved in armed gangs that even the security company personnel were understandably hesitant about risking their lives when responding to a 'call out'. More and more doctors were leaving the country and medication became scarce. I had a friend who needed some heart medication which was unavailable and she had to make a plan to source it in South Africa and then have it transported into Zimbabwe. With the escalating rate of inflation it became obvious that I would need to bring money in from UK just in order to live and, as I was officially retired, I reluctantly agreed to move. In January 2004 I embarked on wrapping up 32 years of my life.

The first decision I had to make was whether to settle in Cape Town or Nelspruit as I wanted to be near one of my immediate family. The volume of traffic in the former is terrific and I wasn't sure that I would be happy driving there, also the Cape winters are cold, wet and windy whereas the Nelspruit climate is similar to that of Mutare. Nelspruit it was to be.

Selling and packing up a house after 32 years is no joke, even for anyone able bodied, and I really struggled. I showed so many prospective buyers over the property, pointing out all the advantages, productivity of the garden, fruit trees etc. that I began to wonder why on earth I was selling.

After many false starts the house was sold to someone who wanted the garden maintained and, to my relief, decided to employ my gardener, Isaac, as I had taught him the basics. Faustina was ready to retire and I was able to pay her a pension so everyone was happy.

Sorting out cupboards in the boys' bedroom I unearthed pieces of shrapnel so carefully collected during the war and other childhood treasures, all quite emotional. I decided to sell a lot of the furniture and that worked out really well. Faustina's daughters had all married well and they wound up buying virtually everything I had to sell. That was such a blessing as it meant that I didn't have strangers wandering through my house. Faustina had built herself a house on the outskirts of Mutare so I gave her my fridge and items of furniture to set her up.

My farewells at school were very emotional. I wasn't sure how I would cope with retirement as teaching had been my life for so long. What a blessing to work beyond retirement age and still enjoy what you are doing! Of course there was endless paper work to be done, getting tax clearance, cancelling car and house insurance as well as the documentation involved in selling the house, the list went on and on. My friend Lyn is a very efficient businesswoman and she was a tower of strength in getting it all organised.

In order to emigrate to South Africa I had to get police clearance from UK, Zambia and Zimbabwe. The first two didn't present any problems but for Zimbabwe I had to be fingerprinted at the police station. That involved two abortive visits when there was no one qualified to take my prints. On my third visit my friend Ann, who was helping me, and I were directed to an open outside garage where there was an old school desk with a South African car number plate resting on it. The finger print ink was poured onto the number plate and I had to roll my fingers and thumbs on it. I could not believe the casual way that the whole exercise was carried out, particularly as I had to pay a considerable sum to have my hands inked with no option to wash them afterwards!

As the time of departure approached I became more and more stressed and it was a huge relief to me when Andy and Jo said they would drive up in Andy's Land Rover to spend the final week with me. Faustina took charge of packing the kitchen goods and when I finally unpacked in Nelspruit she had included some nuts from my Macadamia tree as well as other little items that I had planned to leave behind. The boys kept an eye on the men from the removal company as they packed, which was a great help and they supported me in my farewell get-together.

I had two dogs, Sheba, a Rottweiller, and Jock, a small, old Jack Russell cross who was deaf and becoming blind. I knew that Jock would not happily move to anyone else and nor would he be able to cope with Andy's big dogs so Jo took him to the vet, to be put to sleep – another sad parting. Shortly after I moved in with Andy, Sheba was diagnosed with bone cancer and to my great sadness she was also put to sleep.

All too soon the day of our departure dawned and the grief I felt was almost a physical pain in my heart. Faustina and I were both in floods of tears as we hugged each other. She had been my wonderful helper and friend for 23 years. Even now the thought of my home and friends that I left behind makes me tearful. Jo insisted on driving my car for me, with Sheba in the back, and Andy drove the Land Rover loaded with luggage. We spent the night at the Lion and Elephant Motel as usual and early next morning headed for the border. I sat in the car with Sheba while the boys dealt with the documentation. At one point a customs official came to the door and exclaimed, "You have a live dog in the back of your car !" as though I was unaware of it.

For about a month after I arrived at Andy's home I would suddenly dissolve into tears for no apparent reason. Only when I began to unwind did I come to realise how stressful life in Zimbabwe had been. Within four months I had retired, packed up and sold my home, and was now in a new country with no a place of my own. This was the third time that I had moved to a new country but as one gets older such changes become more difficult.

"I will say of the Lord,' He is my refuge and my fortress, my God, in whom I trust'"

Psalm 91 v 2

I stayed with Andy for nine months whilst I was house hunting in Nelspruit. His property was 30 kilometres from the city with no near neighbours so I was quite lonely at first. Claire and Donavon were both boarders at their private schools and came home most weekends so I was able to help a bit with transporting them. Andy had a ramp put into his swimming pool a while before I arrived so I could have my daily swim.

I arrived in Nelspruit on the 2nd of April having left Faustina planning to move into her new house. At the end of May I received an e-mail telling me that she had been unwell and was diagnosed with liver cancer. It was a great shock as her scan the previous February had been clear. I spoke to her on the phone as she went to stay with her daughter Georgina. She was anxious to reassure me, "Don't worry Madam, I will be fine." She died in August. Such sadness for those left behind but now she is free of pain in heaven, of that I am sure. I am still in touch with her daughters who are all married and now have families of their own.

Although I had visited South Africa so frequently it took me time to adjust to the fact that so many goods were available in the shops all the time. For example there was a huge variety of fresh bread available daily, whereas in Zimbabwe people phoned to let friends know when any loaf was on sale, –

even then, by the time one arrived at the store, the supplies would often have been bought up by the black marketeers. Supplies of cooking oil, flour, sugar and mealie meal (the staple food of black Zimbabweans) were erratic and those engaged in the black market made immense profits, often aided by the police. In Zim. it was often said that if one saw a queue it would be wise to join it as undoubtedly it signalled a supply of something one needed!

With all the ingredients available I was again able to cook which had been my hobby. However, working in the kitchen at Andy's was very frustrating because it was all built-in cupboards and I couldn't get my knees under anything. In the end I bought a collapsible plastic table and that worked well. Don, being a teenager, had a voracious appetite and I had requests to make endless supplies of biscuits and Cornish pasties. Kitchen organisation is very important for a paraplegic. The height of surfaces and ovens, as well as knee room, can be a problem. When Jo and Gee lived in Durban they had a hob that my knees would go under. It was a real joy to be able to cook on open plates where I could see what I was doing, instead of sitting sideways to the stove and stirring blindly, just lifting the saucepan down from time to time to see what was happening. I have now had my own kitchen in Nelspruit reorganised in the same way and it makes cooking so much easier. Previously in my homes I always made a lot of use of an electric frying pan on a low formica-topped table but that isn't as efficient. Now, in their Cape Town home, Jo and Gee have refurbished the kitchen and, as Gee is tall, all the surfaces are high which means that I am unable to help.

When I arrived at Andy's I knew only two people outside my family, Jenny and Di. They are both younger than me and they took me under their wings. Jenny is a nurse and she and her husband, Chris, have become good friends. After a few weeks Di took me as a guest to her book club meeting. While I was there I asked whether any one knew of a 'giggle bridge' group and Valerie took my phone number, saying she would be in touch. From then on I have played bridge at least once a week and now host two tables in my home every Monday afternoon. When I say giggle bridge I mean social bridge. We are all over 60 and enjoy the mental stimulation and company without taking it too seriously.

In 2005 Valerie and I played in a bridge drive which was being held in aid of setting up a hospice in Nelspruit. At the drive volunteers were called for to join the committee. I am not generally a committee person but was dismayed to hear that the neighbouring town of White River which is smaller than Nelspruit had an active hospice whereas Nelspruit didn't, just because people were reluctant to join a committee. As a result I volunteered and served for a year as treasurer. Now the Nelspruit Hospice is well established largely due to the drive of Mary, the president. I am still invited to their social events although I am no longer on the committee.

When I had settled in with Andy I began to attend St Michael's Anglican Church and it was a real joy. The minister, Tony Farrell, and the members of the congregation were so warm and welcoming that I felt as though I had found a whole new family. Just after I had joined St Michael's, Andy took me to Pretoria to consult the shoulder specialist as I was having a great deal of pain in my right shoulder. I had X-rays and a scan and the specialist said my shoulder was partially dislocated and altogether a mess. His conclusion was that I needed a shoulder replacement but he couldn't guarantee how much strength it would give me for lifting. I am very right handed and that shoulder does most of my lifting so I was devastated, the future looked very bleak as I contemplated being even more disabled.

On the following Sunday I spoke to Tony before the service asking if he would pray with me afterwards and he agreed. I was quite embarrassed when at the end of the service he asked for a few volunteers to join him in praying for me. After the congregation left about eight people stayed behind. These were people whom I did not know at that stage and they prayed so fervently and caringly that I was deeply humbled. There was no immediate change but from that time on the pain reduced and my mobility increased. My shoulder has now been pain-free for over five years and I thank God for answering those prayers.

While I was staying with Andy we went to the game farm for several visits and I loved it. On one occasion Jackie and Richard were over from England when we went to the farm. Jackie was keen to overfly the area in a micro-light owned by someone in Hoedspruit, the nearby town. He landed on the farm air strip and took her for a spin and she returned very excited.

I was observing all this from the front seat of the game-viewing vehicle when Andy came over, picked me up in his arms and deposited me on the single passenger seat of the micro-light. I was taken completely by surprise as he put the helmet on my head and the pilot took off with my feet swinging freely in the breeze. It was the most amazing experience, not being enclosed in any way and seeing the animals from the air. If I had time to anticipate the flight I think I would have been nervous about taking to the air in such a flimsy looking machine but it was a real thrill.

House hunting in Nelspruit presented much the same problem as it had in Mutare. The city is also situated in a valley and the suburbs are mainly on the surrounding hill slopes. Again most of the houses are either split level with narrow passages or the gardens have steep slopes. I explained carefully what I needed to the estate agents but nevertheless one took me to a house with five steep steps between the living and the bedroom areas. When I pointed out that it wasn't really suitable he looked very taken aback and said, "Of course you don't notice steps when you can walk." Surely anyone would notice five steps in the middle of a house!

I finally found a single-storey house with three bedrooms and a wider than normal passage. There were only two snags. The first was that I couldn't even get into the bathroom en suite as there was a built-in wash basin unit just inside the doorway. That proved to be a blessing in disguise because I had the whole bathroom reorganised with a shower and bench and the toilet raised to the same height as my chair. My very first bathroom designed for me – such luxury! The second snag was that there was no swimming pool but there was room to put one in. Andy helped design it in such a way that I now have a short ramp which involves much less stress on my shoulders when getting out.

Only after I had bought the house did I hear that after I had made an offer someone else had come along and offered more. Apparently the owner's wife prayed about it and then said to her husband that she was sure it was supposed to be my house so they turned down the other offer. I am so thankful as I am really happy here and can be independent. There are quarters on the property for Lena, my domestic worker, so she lives there but when she goes home I can manage everything for myself.

When I first moved in I had a problem finding someone suitable to help me and was beginning to feel rather panicky about it. The Lord answered my prayers and along came Lena who is, like Faustina, a Christian and very kind and caring. I also employ a gardener twice a week. One of his first tasks was to make a small vegetable garden where I grow lettuces, tomatoes and other salad ingredients as well as beans etc. Still a good Zimbabwean!

When Sheba was put to sleep Andy bought me a German shepherd puppy. I named her Trudi after my very good friend and colleague in Zimbabwe. I then also acquired a small dachsy X Jack Russell bitch called Tinks so I have plenty of company and feel secure.

I had one great thrill while I was still staying with Andy. From the time of my accident I had never been able to go shopping on my own as I always needed someone to take my chair out of the car and I had never lived anywhere where shops were wheelchair friendly, there were always steps. There is a large shopping mall in Nelspruit with car guards patrolling the parking area. Once in the mall everything is on the level. I drove there on my own, recruited a guard to take my chair out and went shopping with a back pack slung over the back of my chair for purchases. You cannot imagine the thrill of browsing around the shops without being anxious about holding someone up, stopping for a cup of coffee just when I felt like it and generally being independent. Of course I have now been several times on my own but it is also good to have company!

In South Africa there are facilities for the disabled which were totally lacking in Zimbabwe. In virtually every parking area there are bays for those using wheelchairs. Able-bodied people who park in these areas illegally fail to realise that the bays are wider than normal to allow the driver or passenger to open the vehicle door to its fullest extent so that a wheelchair can be pushed alongside. There are also toilets in shopping malls and even in the National Parks which are modified for the disabled and make life much more comfortable.

CHAPTER **18**

"Even to your old age and grey hairs I am he, I am he who will sustain you. I have made you and I will carry you, I will sustain you and I will rescue you."

Isaiah 46 v 4

Once I had unpacked and settled into my new home I volunteered to host a church house group as long as someone else would lead it. Tony leapt at the offer and led us for a couple of months before saying that I was now on my own! This was something new for me as facilitating adults is very different from leading the Scripture Union group at school. In fact it has proved a great blessing as I have learnt so much in preparing the studies and it means some teaching skills are involved which mitigated, to some extent, my sense of loss on retirement. Now I also host and lead an inter-denominational Bible study group.

I have always been an avid reader and had hoped to join a book club. Very soon after I became disabled I realised that it was sensible to carry a book with me when going out with passengers. Sometimes they would just need to go into a building with steps or when sightseeing it might be difficult for the chair. If I had a book to read I did not sit there twiddling my thumbs and perhaps feeling resentful. The problem is that most of the book clubs in Nelspruit take turns in meeting at different houses, many of which are not wheelchair friendly. I was bemoaning this one day when a friend said, "Why not start your own and meet at your house?" Why not indeed? I made a number of phone calls and now the club has been running for four years. We have ten members and enjoy our monthly get-togethers and the fact that we have a large variety of books from which to choose.

With weekly bridge and Bible study groups and monthly garden club and book club I keep very busy. That is important to me but the biggest bonus is making new friends. It is not always easy to get to know people when you cannot play sport or move around totally independently.

A major disaster occurred soon after I moved into my house. I was sitting in my car in town waiting for a friend when a young man opened the car door and snatched my handbag. My car still had Zimbabwean registration and a disabled sticker on the windscreen so I was fair game. Not only did I lose my passport, money and cell phone but, worst of all, my Zimbabwe driver's licence. As a result of the last I had to start from scratch to get a South African licence. That involved a written test for a provisional licence and then a road test. When you have been driving for over fifty years that is no joke! I heaved a huge sigh of relief when I finally had a new licence in my hand.

In 2006 I began to have trouble with my first two fingers and thumbs becoming numb on both hands. I also woke with pain in my arms during the night. When it reached the point where doing up buttons and sewing by hand became a problem I went to see an orthopaedic surgeon. He diagnosed carpal tunnel syndrome which necessitated operations on both hands. I opted to have both done at the same time as I really need the use of both to function properly so it would mean shorter recovery time overall. I was in hospital for only a day and Joyce, one of Andy's domestic workers, came and helped Lena for a fortnight, by which time I was able to manage with minimal assistance. A friend took the stitches out for me and I was thoroughly spoilt with friends from the church visiting and bringing ready-cooked meals and flowers. The operation was a complete success.

In June 2007 Andy moved to Cape Town so now I am again without family nearby but at least we are all living in the same country and we are able to visit one another. When Lena goes on leave I fly to Cape Town and stay with Jo, Gee and the children so I also have chance to share in their activities. Gee works three mornings a week and when she is off is very good about taking me out. Favourite haunts are Kirstenbosch Gardens at the foot of Table Mountain or a wheelchair friendly path along the coast. Gee loves shopping so we have jaunts to the hugely expanded Cape Town Waterfront. At weekends the whole family manages at least one trip visiting the wine farms, still as lush and beautiful as when I first saw them from the train in 1959. Now Andy and Sonja have organised a bedroom and bathroom downstairs suitable for me so I am able to share with both families and occasionally to have my entire family around me which is such a joy.

Andy, Jo and their mutual friend, Gavin, built a holiday home on Thesen Islands in Knysna on the south-east coast and it was finished in 2005. When building it they designed a ground floor bedroom and bathroom where I can cope so I have been able to share several holidays with them there. They also have a motor boat into which they lift me to travel around the lagoon. On my last visit Donavon proved his strength by lifting me in for the first time! I am very spoilt by my family.

Among my Nelspruit friends the Botha, Tredgold and Vinson families have been amazing. They have opened their homes to me and treated me like extended family. In addition Lindsay has undertaken the maintenance of my wheelchairs and the swimming pool, while Ken has sorted out various other mechanical and electrical problems. Men seem to have an innate understanding of mechanics which I, and I think most women, lack.

There are times when things which are easy for most people are difficult, if not impossible, for me. Recently my house alarm malfunctioned and I couldn't turn it off. The security man on call said he couldn't come out and told me what to do. That was fine except I couldn't reach the relevant wire in the control box in order to disconnect it. It was after eleven at night and I was supremely conscious of the alarm blaring and disturbing every human and dog in the neighbourhood. In desperation I phoned Ken who kindly came to my rescue.

On another occasion my gardener climbed on the roof of the house in order to pick avocados for himself. When we had the next shower of rain it was about eleven thirty at night and I awoke to find my bed soaking wet as water was leaking through the ceiling. Now what? On that occasion I phoned Lindsay and he came over and moved my bed away from the deluge. Subsequently it transpired that several tiles on the roof had been broken. I am eternally grateful for the help and support I receive. When reading about the gloom and doom in the world it really restores one's faith in mankind to experience such kindness.

I am often asked how I managed to adjust to becoming a paraplegic and I can only reply, "With the Lord's help." I get frustrated at times, particularly when things are put out of my reach. Once in a while I have sat in my car and enviously watched people walking past but it doesn't do to dwell on it. Quite recently I dreamt that I stood up and was amazed at how different the world looked from that height – all very strange as I usually dream walking anyhow! I just know that I have been blessed in so many ways and that there are people walking around whose hidden burdens are greater than mine. People all have their down times and I am no different but I am aware of being very blessed.

Jo tells me that according to modern theory I belong to the Silent Generation who were born from 1920 to 1940 and lived through either the depression or the Second World War. Apparently we are hard working, we have a waste not, want not mentality and hate getting into debt. I would agree with all of that but would also add that we are a coping generation rather than expecting a lot to be done for us.

Now, at 73, I give thanks for each day as it comes. I realise that my independence could vanish overnight if my weakened shoulders no longer allow me to lift my weight. At the same time I know that many of my friends also face problems as ageing bodies let them down. An American friend always says, "Old age isn't for wimps," which is as true for the able-bodied as for the disabled.

My life has turned out very differently from anything I could have envisaged in Christmas 1959. Ouma's predictions were uncannily accurate, especially the one saying that I would be immensely blessed. As I look back over almost 51 years as a paraplegic I know that becoming disabled does not signal an end to a full and meaningful existence. I am so grateful for the varied life and joy that God has given me and know there are still more treats in store. Next year there are plans for a trip to England and Switzerland with Jo and the family so that is something more to anticipate.

The Lord has sustained me to my old age and grey hair and blessed me with a wonderful family and friends – how could I not feel overcome with gratitude?